BEGINNER'S GUIDE TO
COIN COLLECTING

BEGINNER'S GUIDE TO
COIN COLLECTING

Ted Schwarz

Dolphin Books
DOUBLEDAY & COMPANY, INC., Garden City, New York
1980

The author wishes to thank Krause Publications in Iola, Wisconsin, and the American Numismatic Association in Colorado Springs, Colorado, for their help in supplying photographs.

Library of Congress Cataloging in Publication Data

Schwarz, Theodore.
Beginner's guide to coin collecting.

Bibliography: p. 136.
1. Coins—Collectors and collecting. I. Title.
CJ81.S37   737.4′075
ISBN: 0-385-14491-1

Library of Congress Catalog Card Number 78–22353

CONTENTS

BEGINNER'S GUIDE TO
COIN COLLECTING

Chapter 1

THE STORY OF COINS

The next time you buy a newspaper, pay for a soft drink, or count the change needed for a bus ride, take a closer look at the coins you have in your hand. Everyone knows they are tools of the business world, but did you know that coins can tell stories, reveal the world's great art treasures, and serve as a miniature history lesson? Coin collectors know this, and their hobby is one of the most exciting you can enjoy. In fact, since you can easily collect coins dating back two thousand years and more, you might one day hold in your hand a coin used by Alexander the Great as he conquered the known world or a coin buried by the pirate Captain Kidd after he looted a treasure ship.

Coin designs are not only beautiful, they also provide glimpses of the ancient wonders of the world, long since disappeared. The Circus Maximus, the magnificent Roman arena where chariot races and athletic contests were held, was altered by various rulers and even destroyed by fire at one time. Yet each architectural change is visible through the coinage of ancient Rome. Statues destroyed by earthquakes, fires, and the ravages of time retain their full majestic beauty on the surfaces of coins.

Coins have also been the subject of humorous stories over the years. When a new type of U.S. five-cent piece was introduced in 1883, a deaf mute named Josh Tatum gold-plated the coins and took them to cigar stores. The coin had only the roman numeral "V" to show its value; it didn't indicate dollars or cents. He would point to a five-cent cigar and give a gold-plated five-cent piece in payment. If the owner recognized the coin, he'd thank Josh, who would then depart. However, the owner usually thought the coin was a $5.00 gold piece and gave Josh $4.95 in change. Tatum left with the extra money, a fact that eventually resulted in his being brought to trial. The publicity of that trial, where he was acquitted, introduced a new word into our language. Whenever someone pulls a trick on someone, gets caught, and doesn't want the victim to think he was being malicious, it is common for the person to say he was "just joshing."

Some coin collectors save only those coins that were used in ways the mint never intended. A coin from colonial America punched with a hole and bearing teeth marks was probably used as a necklace good-luck charm to protect a teething baby from witches. Copper one-cent pieces have been notched to serve as gun stocks on frontiersmen's rifles. Large copper cents have been cut to serve as valve cocks, shaved and numbered to act as hotel-room key holders, and tossed in pickle barrels to turn the cucumbers a beautiful shade of green. Unfortunately, this latter approach to pickle-making causes a chemical reaction that poisons anyone eating the pickles, a fact that ended this once-popular use.

Some collectors do not save coins at all but only those items that have served as coin substitutes. Salt was used as money in the Ohio Valley and elsewhere. Soap was used to pay bills in Mexico, and bricks of tea paid for food and shelter in China at one time. On the island of Yap, stone wheels of various sizes have served as money. A twelve-inch stone wheel was worth about seventy-five dollars, and a wealthy elder might have a stone wheel twelve feet across to show his great worth.

Coins have been used by men and women throughout the world for more than two thousand years, and there are written records of coin collectors dating back more than fifteen hundred years. This makes coin collecting one of the oldest hobbies enjoyed by large numbers of people.

There was a time when it was impossible to collect coins because there was no such thing as money. People lived in small communities, isolated from one another. They bartered for what they needed, relying upon the goods and services in their immediate area. For example, suppose a man who raised chickens needed a new pair of shoes. He would go to the shoemaker and offer to trade one or more of his chickens for the shoes he desired. If the shoemaker liked chicken, he would agree to the arrangement. If he did not, the man with the chickens might have to trade them to another

farmer for a cow and then offer the cow to the shoemaker. The system was crude but effective.

As communities grew larger, tools and weapons became standards by which all other items were judged. Everyone needed tools and weapons, so it was easy to decide that one chicken was worth a certain number of axes. The same was true for shoes, clothing, and other necessary items. Thus the chicken farmer could bring an ax to the shoemaker, who would accept it and later use it to pay for the cow he wanted. This was especially helpful when trade relations were established between nearby communities.

Later cattle were used as the standard rate of payment. A day's labor might be worth a half cow, or a large vegetable harvest might be worth ten cows. The only problem was that cattle came in all sizes and shapes. No one could decide if a fat cow should be worth the same as a thin cow. Even when an agreement was reached, there was still the problem of some of the poor people having no place to graze the cow when it was offered in payment and nevertheless not wanting to slaughter it.

The domestication of the horse provided a major boost toward the creation of coinage. When people could ride, they were able to travel farther and longer than ever thought possible. People living in one part of the world were no longer isolated from those hundreds of miles away. They were exposed to new ways of bartering and systems of money. What was good in one area was scorned in another. The Hittites wanted to use cattle as their medium of exchange, but the Egyptians offered gold, silver, bronze, and electrum, a mixture of silver and gold found in nature. The people of Cyprus wanted neither approach, as they relied on copper ingots.

The period of exploration and conquest by mounted soldiers began around 100 B.C. Caravans of traders traveled the roads two hundred years later. And everywhere there was the problem of finding a common medium of exchange.

The ancient Greeks developed an early money device based on a combination of the use of precious metals and the animal-barter approach. Copper and bronze miniature models of oxhides were made, each piece of metal being the value of one ox. One bronze or copper oxhide was known as a talent, with several such pieces called talanton.

Then weights were substituted for barter objects. A very large weight was worth one ox. Smaller weights were worth portions of the animals.

Ingots of gold, silver, and other metals became valuable objects that had to be stored when accumulated in quantity. Special treasure houses, usually in sacred temples or palaces, were utilized by Kings and merchants to hold their ingots. Clay tablets were used by the guards to maintain records of royal and business transactions. Yet none of these valued ingots were actually coins as we know them.

During all this development of precious-metal use, another aspect of coinage—design—was developing. At least as early as 2250 B.C., special seals were used when signing important documents, adding emblems, etc. Sometimes the seals were worn on rings called signet rings. Other times they were carved into cylinders and called cylinder seals. In every case, the seals had special designs unique to the person using the device.

Around 700 B.C., in a West Asia Minor country known as Lydia, the people decided to combine a number of business concepts into what evolved into coinage. They used the small designs of the signet rings and cylinder seals to denote authority and stamped them into lumps of precious metal that represented set values. They used ideas pulled from Persia, Assyria, Egypt, and other countries whose goods were traded in the Lydian capital of Sardis.

The first coins as we know them were struck about 640 B.C. under the Lydian King Ardys. No one knows who had the idea for the coins. They were extremely crude in appearance and made from pieces of electrum.

One side of the new coins had a design punched into the surface. The other side had a rough pattern of lines. Apparently the pieces of electrum were placed on an anvil (thus the pattern of lines) and struck with a punch formed into the design seen in the coins.

After some forty years of coinage, Lydia changed the way it made its money. A die was made for each side, the metal resting on one side while being struck with the other. The designs were also improved and, by the time King Alyattes came to power, in the period of around 615 through 560 B.C., a legend was added reading "I am the mark of Phanes." The man named Phanes is believed to have been a wealthy merchant or early banker who was backing the coins with his personal or business holdings.

The early Lydian coins were not official government issues, though the people from all corners of the country used the coins at set values. It took King Croesus, who ruled Lydia from 560 to 546 B.C., to issue the first coins guaranteed by the government. These were considered to be the first coins as we know them today in that they were official government issues.

Croesus also changed the metallic content of coins. He banned the use of electrum because the ratio of gold to silver varied greatly. Electrum was found in nature but not with a consistent gold/silver pattern. He insisted that only pure gold or pure silver be utilized in the future.

Persia conquered Lydia during Croesus' rule, thus spreading the knowledge of coinage to an ever-wider area. The Persian conquerors eventually reached Chaldea, Babylonia, parts of Greece, and Asia Minor, among other territories. They brought with them a version of coinage based upon the Lydian concept.

This is the front and back of one of the earliest coins, a stater of Attica. It features a sea turtle with smooth shell on the obverse, a symbol of Aegina, who was supposedly watching over the land. The reverse has a simple incuse or stamped design of four triangles. This coin dates back to before 550 B.C.

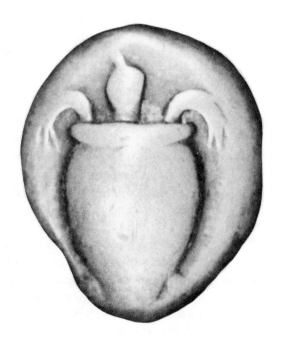

The ancient Greeks were master craftsmen and expert engravers of intricate objects on tiny gemstones. They found the method of striking coins developed by the Lydians to be artistically crude. They decided to use intricately carved figures of birds, fish, and animals for their designs. These represented old barter objects and helped the people of the various Greek city-states make the transition to coinage. Thus the coins of Aegina show a turtle shell since the sea turtle's shell was a valued barter object. Cows were on the gold talent for reasons already mentioned, and a wine cup was shown on coins from the isle of Naxos, where measures of wine were the medium of exchange.

A few of the city-states used objects that were puns—plays on the name of the area. The table (trapeza) was used on the coins of Trapezos. The rose is known as Rhodes and the elbow (known as an ankon) is shown on the coins of Ankona.

The Greeks were not satisfied with their coins, however. In the fifth century B.C. they produced more elaborate figures and within the next hundred years were using designs showing people and animals in action. The Greeks also added works of art and architectural triumphs to their coins. The Colossus of Rhodes, a statue of the sun god Helios that was more than one hundred feet high and stood atop the harbor at Rhodes, was placed in miniature on ancient Greek coins. The Colossus succumbed to the devastating destructive force of an earthquake in 224 B.C., but we know how it looked, more than two thousand years after its destruction, because of the coins on which it was reproduced.

During the centuries there were other changes as well. Starting with the sixth century B.C., coin designs, either on one or both sides, were raised instead of being stamped into the coins.

Perhaps the most famous of all Greek coins were those of the trade center in Athens. The coins had the image of an owl on them and they were so respected that traders took them to the far corners of the known world. These were introduced in 556 B.C. by the ruler Pesistratus.

This is one of the famous owls of Athens. It was used in the period around 430 to 332 B.C.

Coin designs continued to evolve. The ancient Romans utilized coins as educational devices for the public. Every coin has two sides —the front or "heads" side, known to collectors as the "obverse," and the back or "tails" side, known as the "reverse." With Roman coins, the ruler's head was always shown on the obverse of the coin. If two people appeared, one on the obverse and one on the reverse, the figure on the obverse was known to be the person in charge.

Because of this approach to coinage, we know some unusual facts about the Romans. For example, although women were not respected outside the home and normally did not enter politics, Nero's mother, Agrippina, managed to so influence her son that, for one year of his reign, she was an equal ruler with him. During that year her profile can be seen

on the obverse, right along with her son's. She used a combination of trickery, flattery, and even incest to hold the position during that year but lost favor later in his rule. Her portrait on the later coins was relegated to the reverse.

The Romans also used their coins to tell of battles won, buildings constructed, and athletic events held. They were the newspaper "capsule commentaries" of their day.

Today coins come with all manner of designs. American coins have been used to honor famous leaders in recent years. We have a half dollar honoring President Kennedy, a dollar honoring President Eisenhower, and other denominations honoring Thomas Jefferson, Abraham Lincoln, Franklin Roosevelt, and George Washington.

Other countries use coins to show some part of their history. Canadian silver dollars have designs that reveal aspects of Canada's heritage as well as honoring the British monarchs. A totem-pole design on one Canadian dollar tells of the Indian heritage of the nation. In a different year, the dollar design showed a Northwest Mounted Police officer sitting astride his horse. A third design from yet another year shows a cowboy riding a bucking bronco, part of the heritage of the Canadian West.

Coins from European nations honor rulers, musicians, birds, animals, and numerous other topics. Some collectors make a specialty of collecting only coins with animals or only coins featuring famous women. Such collectors buy their coins according to the topic of the design and are known as topical collectors.

But what coins should you use to start your collection? How do you choose from the thousands of different types of coins that are seen in different countries of the world?

Since coins are money, many people assume you have to be wealthy to collect them. Fortunately this is not the case. You can start your collection by sorting through pocket change and saving the different Lincoln cents you find. Or you might buy packets of inexpensive foreign coins from nations whose money is worth only a fraction of our dollar. Many dealers offer foreign coins for prices of just one or two cents each. These will never be valuable from an investor's viewpoint but they are worth their weight in gold in the pleasure, the history, and the richness of art they impart.

The amount of use a coin has seen will also be a factor in determining its cost. The more a coin has circulated, going from hand to pocket to cash register and back, the less desirable it is to collectors. A coin collector looks for specific signs of wear, to be discussed in detail later in this book, when determining the value of that coin. If a coin is "uncirculated"—exactly as it came from the mint before it could be used as change—a collector will pay more money than for a coin that has been used. Some coins can be purchased for just a few cents each when well worn. These are fun to own, quite beautiful, and far more reasonable than that same coin uncirculated, which might cost hundreds of dollars. Thus a coin that is a great rarity in uncirculated condition can be

owned by a low-budget collector when that coin has been worn through wide use.

Wear is the result of rubbing a coin receives, including the rubbing that comes from your handling of a piece from your collection. Thus it is important that you always hold a coin by the outer rim. When not in use, the coins should be stored by one of the methods mentioned later in this book. They should not just be tossed together in a box or drawer, because they can rub and scratch each other.

Most collectors start by saving the coins from their own country, since these are readily available. United States collectors generally start with coins from circulation, then select earlier issues, no longer available in pocket change, for which they pay a premium of anywhere from a few cents to thousands of dollars if the coin is rare. Canadians start with the coins of Canada, then frequently branch to issues from Great Britain, the mother country. Mexicans save their nation's pesos, and so it goes around the world. But before you decide how you want to plan your collection, let's take a general look at all the coins of the world, starting with those of the United States.

Chapter 2

UNITED STATES COINS

The earliest money in the United States was a variety of barter objects relied upon by the first colonists. Animal skins were valued highly, with a male deerskin (a "buck") valued at one (Spanish) dollar. The Virginia and Maryland colonies used powder and shot, essential for their rifles, as means of making payment. In Connecticut, community service was required as payment for taxes. The men would build bridges, public buildings, and handle the other needs of the colony instead of paying tax money for someone to be hired to do the work.

Wampum was probably the most famous colonial money. The Indians took shells and polished them until they were the size of beads, then holed and strung them for easy handling. They were white and blue, with the blue worth approximately twice the white. A British penny was worth from four to eight beads, depending upon where it was offered. This worked well at first because the supply was kept limited by the Indians. However, the white men began manufacturing wampum in quantity and some unscrupulous colonists dyed the white shells blue, all of which led to inflation and a lessening of value.

Food and tobacco were also popular money crops. Tobacco could be traded in the Carolinas, Pennsylvania, and New Jersey, among other colonies. New Hampshire relied on fish for much of its "money," and New Jersey, Pennsylvania, and others often used corn, wheat, and similar crops.

The coins available to the colonists were as varied as the people living in the Americas. New Spain, now Mexico, had a mint as early as 1536, more than 80 years before the earliest British colonial settlement to the north. Coins such as the real—roughly 12½ cents—were issued. These coins were known as "bits," with two bits eventually to equal the American quarter dollar—not to mention a shave and a haircut. An 8-real coin was the equivalent of the American dollar. These eventually became the famous "pieces of eight" of pirate lore.

The early British colonists were not permitted to strike their own coins: This was the exclusive privilege of the King or anyone whom he delegated. Unfortunately, this meant a severe coin shortage in America. The colonists had very limited cargo space on the small ships they sailed to the new land. Weight was a problem, food and supplies taking prece-

Spanish silver dollars were among the most important coins utilized in commerce during the colonial periods of the United States, Canada, and Mexico.

dence over the coins. What few coins were brought to the colonies were usually returned almost immediately in payment for new tools, furniture, and other items imported from the mother country.

The people of the Massachusetts colony re-

alized that coins were going to be essential for them to do business in their community. They had reales from the mint in New Spain, wampum, a few British pounds, and a handful of coins from France and other countries whose adventurers were exploring North America. But the numbers were limited and the variety too great for standardizing on coinage. There was also tremendous resentment against the Crown for denying the colonists the right to produce necessity coinage.

The result, on May 26, 1652, was the first act of the American Revolution, though none of the people realized this at the time. The Massachusetts colonists authorized a silversmith named John Hull to start a mint for the coining of shillings, sixpence, and threepence. The coins were to be of a lower silver content than the equivalent British coins, since the devaluation would make them undesirable to British merchants. This would prevent the new pieces from being exported in payment for merchandise the colonists ordered from time to time.

These first coins were crudely struck. Most of the coin was blank, with the obverse having just the initials "NE" stamped on the surface and the reverse having the Roman numerals "XII," "VI," or "III," depending upon the denomination. The coins were unevenly shaped and the dishonest among the colonists found they could scrape or clip small sections of the coin to obtain bits of silver. The coins could still be spent at face value since the damage wasn't readily noticeable. The shaved silver was accumulated, melted, and used for its intrinsic worth.

On October 19, 1652, Hull changed the design, making it more elaborate. A willow tree was placed in the center of the obverse with the words "IN MASATHVSETS" surrounding it. The reverse bore the date and the denomination number in the center and the words "NEW ENGLANDANDOM" surrounding it. Later, oak and pine-tree designs were made. In every case, so much of the sur-

These are the early New England coins that John Hull produced for the colonists in defiance of the Crown. Many of these coins were shoveled into a balance until they equaled the weight of his daughter when he was preparing her dowry.

face of the coin was utilized that unnoticeable clipping was no longer possible.

King Charles II became irate when he first learned of the Massachusetts coinage. However, Sir Thomas Temple, representing the colonists' interests, managed to appease him by lying about the design. When Charles II's palace was attacked by Lord Cromwell, the King managed to save his own life by climbing an oak tree and hiding in its branches. Temple said the coin showed that very same royal oak and was meant as a tribute to the Crown. The King, touched by the thought, agreed not to take any sanctions against the colonists. The people of Massachusetts protected themselves further by retaining the date "1652" on the coins so the King wouldn't know how long they were made.

John Hull later became famous for the endowment of his daughter, Hannah, when she married Samuel Seawall. He had her sit on one side of a large balance and shoveled pine-tree shillings from his mint into the other side until the weight of the coins equaled the girl's weight. The exact value of the dowry has been lost to history, though estimates go as high as thirty thousand pounds in British money. (The pound is a type of money, not her weight.) Most likely the real figure was around five hundred British pounds, with an initial payment of thirty pounds given to the couple, thirty-five pounds more provided a month later, and the remainder paid several months after the marriage.

Other colonies followed Massachusetts' lead in obtaining coinage, though not in defiance of the Crown. Maryland's coinage, for example, was officially sanctioned. Cecil Calvert, the second Lord Baltimore and "Lord Proprietor of Maryland," had Maryland's coins produced in England specifically for colonial use. This was in 1658.

There were also coins struck for New Jersey, Virginia, and others. In addition, coin substitutes in the form of copper tokens saw circulation.

The Revolutionary War had its own coinage of a sort. These coins were made when the Continental Congress was planning a formal break with England in 1776. The dollar coins were what is known as patterns—coins made as an experiment to see how easily they can be produced, how good they look, etc., but never struck for circulation. Continental dollars have the image of the sun shining down on a sundial and the motto: "FUGIO, MIND YOUR BUSINESS" in the center of the obverse. "CONTINENTAL CURENCY (sic) 1776" on the outside. The reverse has thirteen linking circles, each with the name of a colony. In the center are the words: "AMERICAN CONGRESS, WE ARE ONE." These are known in brass, silver, and pewter.

The obverse (front) and reverse (back) of what was known as a fugio cent. Fugio means "time flies" and the motto reads "Mind Your Business." The mottoes were apparently originated by Benjamin Franklin and the coins have been casually called the Franklin cents. Although the link-and-chain design was used, no complaints were made at this time. The link-and-chain design became a major controversy after it was used for the early large cents.

An example of the Continental dollar, which was probably a pattern issue made in very limited number. These exist in pewter, brass, and silver. They were probably made by Elisha Gallaudet. They are believed to have been struck in Philadelphia, where the Continental Congress was meeting.

Coins of a design similar to the Continental dollars are one-cent pieces known as Fugio cents. They were made by a New York merchant in May of 1787. He obtained official government sanction through bribery and other dishonest means. He was supposed to supply millions of the copper coins to the government but eventually struck just four hundred thousand.

The United States Mint, established in Philadelphia in 1792, got off to a slow start. There were shortages of equipment and supplies including silver, copper, and gold. George Washington took a personal interest in the new mint and was anxious to do whatever he could to get coins into production. In exasperation over the delays caused by a lack of silver, he convinced Martha to give up a family silver tea service. This was melted and coined into five-cent pieces known as half dismes. Ten-cent pieces known as dismes were also struck in silver. The year was 1792 and three different types of cents were prepared as well, including a small copper coin with a piece of silver in the center so the intrinsic value would equal the face value of one cent. These coins are considered patterns, however, as few were struck and fewer still were circulated.

The earliest coins of the U. S. Mint were struck in copper and they included both half cents and large cents. The coin designs almost included the head of George Washington, but he declined such honors. Our nation's first President felt that if his head appeared on the coins, it would seem like a throwback to the coins of a monarchy, and he refused. The bust of a woman, symbol of Liberty, was considered far more appropriate. Unfortunately, the designers for these coins were inexperienced, and the early images of Liberty left much to be desired.

For example, in 1793, the first full year of coinage for the mint, the obverse of the large cent (a copper piece approximately double the diameter of the Lincoln cent found in change today) has a rendering of a woman whose hair flies straight out from her head. She looks as though her body is touching a machine generating static electricity.

Although George Washington did not want his face to appear on U.S. coinage, there were a number of tokens and coins made to honor him by various private individuals. This Washington halfpenny was produced in 1795. It was probably made in England.

The reverse of that first large-cent design has interlocking chain links forming an unbroken ring. Each link represents a state, and the design is quite similar to that of the Continental dollar. Despite the fact that the earlier use was considered noncontroversial, the use of the chain design on the large cent aroused extreme controversy.

The Pennsylvania *Gazette,* a popular newspaper of the day, was shocked by the new coins. According to an item dated March 20, 1793: "The American cents (says a letter from Newark) do not answer our expectations. The chain on the reverse is but a bad omen for liberty, and liberty herself appears to be in a fright. —May she not justly cry out in the words of the Apostle 'Alexander the coppersmith hath done me much harm; the Lord reward him according to his works.'"

The head of Liberty on the large cent was modified slightly that same year and the chain

The large cent of 1793, perhaps the most controversial coin the United States has ever issued. There has never been a worse-looking figure of Liberty used on American coins.

problems. The work was so poor that in 1839, two design modifications were known respectively as the "Silly Head" and the "Booby Head" coins.

For some reason the half-cent series was never plagued with the same problems as the large cent. A wreath was used on the reverse of even the earliest coins and the head of Liberty was always far more attractive.

The evolution of coin design is shown by the numerous varieties that occurred within a few short years. This is a design used on the early silver dollars and half dollars.

was replaced with a wreath. Then, in 1794, a more attractive Liberty head was introduced with a ribbon holding her hair in place. However, the large-cent series, which was struck through 1857, was always plagued with design

Other coins were introduced during those first few years of the mint. "Half dimes," the spelling changed from "disme," were struck in 1794, with "dimes" appearing two years later. Quarter dollars also appeared in 1796, but silver half dollars and dollars were struck in 1794. Five-dollar and $10 gold pieces appeared in 1795, with $2.50 gold pieces struck the following year.

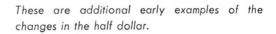

These are additional early examples of the changes in the half dollar.

The obverse of one of the earliest half cents; fortunately the frightened head of Liberty was never tried on any of these coins.

In 1804, the ten-dollar gold piece was introduced with the phrygian cap. This was the cap of freedom worn by slaves who had won the right to be on their own.

In 1831, a rather simple but elegant reverse was added for the half cent.

A variation in the head of Liberty as used on the large cents of the 1830s.

The gold pieces have been nicknamed according to their reverse eagle design. A $10 gold piece is known as an "eagle" to collectors. Everything else is named in relationship to the $10 coin. Thus a $5.00 gold piece is a half eagle, a $2.50 coin is a quarter eagle, and a $20 gold piece is a double eagle.

This early eagle design, used as the reverse on half dollars as early as 1801, was the first heraldic eagle. Prior to that the birds looked as though they were suffering from malnutrition.

Although many of the United States coin designs are illustrated here, this book will be able to touch on the coin history of the United States only briefly. Later you will find information about publications providing in-depth facts on the history and value of almost every country's coins in which you might be interested. For this chapter I will touch on some of the unusual highlights of U.S. coin history only.

In 1837, a number of artists collaborated on a coin design eventually executed by Christian Gobrecht. The design shows a seated figure of Liberty with a shield by her side. The

A more dignified large-cent design than the early chain cent that causes so much controversy.

coins were considered at that time to be the most beautiful designs ever issued by the United States. But though the basic design was beautiful, at least one private citizen felt the need to modify the obverse in a rather unusual manner. It seems that during the 1850s, a cer-tain counterfeiter was frequently in and out of prison. His life was devoted to the illegal production of coinage. When he wasn't in prison, he was busy counterfeiting coins. And when he was serving a sentence, he kept in practice by altering half dollars with tools smuggled into his cell. He took the Seated-Liberty coins and carefully smoothed, then altered the shield. When his work was completed, Miss Liberty appeared to be seated on a chamber pot.

As the United States became settled, Americans moved to new territories in search of riches. Gold and silver were discovered in many parts of the South and West. News of the findings spread around the world and instant towns were created in the areas near the strikes. The California Gold Rush, for example, brought settlers to San Francisco from as far away as Australia. Most men found barely enough gold and/or silver to pay their expenses. But a few in every community hit the giant bonanzas that resulted in their becoming instant millionaires, and this minority success gave hope to the hundreds of others working the same general territory.

At first everyone arriving in a gold- or silver-mining boom town was determined to prospect for riches. They brought all the provisions they thought they would need in order to become wealthy. Letters and diaries kept by some of these individuals indicate that many felt a maximum of thirty days would be enough time to find great wealth, so they only brought along adequate provisions for such a stay.

As the days passed and little gold was found, many men ran out of both supplies and hope. Most returned to their homes back East or in other countries of the world. A few realized that there was more money to be made above the ground than beneath it. They opened stores, bars, brothels, and other businesses to serve the men digging for gold. Prices were high for everything, and in cities where gold was being sought, gold dust in varying amounts was the most acceptable form of payment.

In San Francisco, many merchants took advantage of the gold seekers who created that "boom" city in 1849. Whenever a man wanted to pay for a drink, a meal, or supplies, he would take a pouch of gold dust and open it for the merchant. The merchant would take a "pinch" of gold dust equal to the cost of the item purchased. The exact amount was somewhat arbitrary but usually fairly close to what an accurate weighing of the dust might have indicated was correct. However, the merchants and bartenders made it a point to keep their fingernails long and sticky. They would jam their hands into the bags of dust, letting relatively large amounts stick to their nails in addition to the "pinch" they were legitimately obtaining. When the customer wasn't looking, the merchants would scrape the gold from their nails into a bag kept behind the counter. Many crooked bar owners made two to three times as much money from the periodic cleaning of their nails than they made from the price of their drinks.

Although many of the merchants enjoyed using gold dust as a medium of exchange, it really wasn't a very good coin substitute. The miners and other townspeople were being cheated, and no one was very happy. An effort was made to get regular U. S. Mint issues to the mining towns, but they were usually remote enough that this was difficult or impossible. The prospectors never carried many coins with them, as they needed to travel light, taking only minimal provisions.

The first alternative to gold dust and gold ore as money came with the introduction of tokens to be used as small change. Many of these were brass and valued in a particular commodity from the issuing store. Some were worth a loaf of bread. Others were good for a glass of whiskey. A few were issued in Colorado by the operators of "bawdy houses," whose tokens were good for enjoying the favors of a "wench of ill repute." Many of

these survive to this day, though most of the bawdy-house tokens available from dealers are modern restrikes sold as souvenirs to tourists.

Other tokens were made from gold and had carefully controlled intrinsic worth. North Carolina and South Carolina gold miners relied on gold tokens made by Christopher Bechtler, for example. These were unofficial "coins," most valued at $2.50 or $5.00, the approximate intrinsic worth of the gold used. According to Bechtler's records, he made approximately $2 million in gold-coin substitutes for the people in his region, and these are avidly sought collectors' items today.

Other tokens made from gold, with values like coins struck by the U. S. Mint, were produced by various individuals in areas such as Pike's Peak and Georgia Gulch, Colorado, San Francisco, Utah, and elsewhere. These were all considered to be "necessity coins" and were meant as a temporary measure until the merchants could obtain legal-tender coins.

This period was not the first era when coin substitutes were used. Tokens were issued by merchants during the 1830s when Andrew Jackson was President. A coin shortage and depression led many businesses to issue tokens for use as change, advertising, and political commentary. These were known as "Jackson tokens" or "hard-times tokens." Unlike the tokens made during the gold-rush years, the Jackson pieces were only of base metal, issued in areas where U.S. coins were circulating though in short supply. They were never meant to be a substitute coinage.

The federal government finally decided that certain key areas of the country should have branch mints established. At the branch mints, gold and silver ore taken from the mines could be converted into coinage. This prevented the risk of loss due to shipping and solved local coinage needs to a great degree. During the period from 1849 until shortly after 1900, branch mints were established in Denver, Colorado; San Francisco, California; Carson City, Nevada; New Orleans, Louisiana; Charlotte,

These are examples of various merchant tokens issued during periods of coin shortages. Many of these were politically inspired. The Jackson tokens were meant to ridicule President Andrew Jackson. The token reading "Am I not a woman & a sister" showing a black woman in chains was an early example of a token used in the antislavery campaign. Other tokens just had advertisements for the merchants issuing them.

North Carolina; and Dahlonega, Georgia. The Denver, San Francisco, and Philadelphia mints remain active today, along with a Lincoln-cent-minting facility in West Point, New York. The other mints have all been closed, with two, the one in Dahlonega and the branch in Charlotte, in use only from 1838 to 1861 and then only for gold coins.

Each branch mint is identified by one or two letters, which form what is known as the "mint mark." With the exception of silver "nickels" minted during the Second World War, each of which had a big letter "P" on the reverse when struck at Philadelphia, none of the coins made in the Philadelphia Mint has an identifying letter. All the others do. They include an "S" for San Francisco, a "D" for Denver as well as Dahlonega (the Dahlonega Mint shut down before the Denver Mint was built, so there is no problem in learning which mint produced a particular "D"-marked coin), a "C" for Charlotte, "CC" for Carson City, and an "O" for New Orleans. Later in this book I will show you how to spot the mint mark on different types of coins in detail.

Examples of quarter dollar reverses. The example above was used from 1804 through 1807. The example below was typical of the design used on the reverse of the coins introduced in 1838. This was the original reverse of the Gobrecht quarter dollars and was later modified. This Gobrecht design was repeated on the half dollars, dimes (Seated Liberty only), half dimes, and the dollars.

An example of the very popular Seated-Liberty design engraved by Christian Gobrecht.

San Francisco needed coinage more than most early cities as a result of gold and silver strikes. Everything from food to shelter to clothing was so scarce that prices rose until only the rich could afford more than the basic necessities. One man brought 1,500 dozen eggs to the city and sold them for $3.75 a dozen. This was an enormous profit over his cost and a tremendously high price for the buyer to pay since most men were earning a maximum of $1.00 a day when they were doing well.

The reverse of the gold ten-dollar coin struck by the San Francisco Mint (note small letter "s" directly above the space between the "E" and the "N" in the word "TEN"). The style of reverse was in use from 1866 through 1907. A second reverse was used in 1907 when the Saint-Gaudens design was introduced.

But the person to whom the original merchant sold the eggs immediately marked them up again—to $4.00 a dozen. And people began paying that price.

The first merchant realized what a gold mine he had missed. He bought back the remaining eggs at the $4.00-a-dozen asking price, then resold them all for $6.00 a dozen.

Restaurants catered to the very rich. Delmonico's menu included St. Julian soup for $1.00, boiled salmon trout in anchovy sauce for $1.75, and fillet of beef in mushroom sauce for the same price, among numerous other high-priced offerings. A full meal might cost as much as $5.00, not including beverage and tip. The average family enjoying such a night on the town could spend two to three weeks' normal income for the one Delmonico's meal. Yet enough people were getting rich from gold strikes that Delmonico's was never at a loss for business.

Even before a United States Mint branch was established in San Francisco, the government was so concerned about the coin shortages and the private-mint substitutes in California that a U. S. Government assay office was established. A firm known as Moffat & Company had been unofficially issuing gold coins for use as change during the early 1850s, as had a number of other businesses. These ranged in denomination from $5.00 to $50, with most being in the $10 to $20 range. The federal government made Moffat & Company an official agency that could assay gold, then coin it into $10, $20, and $50 gold pieces whose marked value would be assured by an agency of the U. S. Government. These assay pieces were not the same as coins produced by the mint but had legal-tender status since they could be used to pay all federal debts and taxes. The year was 1852 and the $50 gold pieces thus produced are the largest-denomination coins ever used by this country's business community.

The San Francisco Mint was finally established on April 3, 1854. However, production was slow for the next two years and a number of private issues continued to be used as change until the coin shortage was eliminated.

At the start of the Civil War, people began hoarding all the coins they could find. Silver and gold were packed into jars and hidden in and around people's homes. Even copper

The United States Assay Office produced this fifty-dollar gold piece in 1852. The United States Assay Office was in San Francisco and was the coinage authority immediately prior to the building of the San Francisco Mint.

cents were hidden, a fact that resulted in a serious coin shortage, preventing merchants from being able to make change.

Many merchants who lacked coins returned to the use of tokens. Some were meant to be substitutes for specific coins and had a value stamped on them. Others were good for a loaf of bread or a drink of whiskey, such as had been the case with tokens issued during the gold rush and the silver rush. A man named Alfred Robbinson produced a token in 1861 that read: "Value Me as You Please."

A number of tokens were patriotic. Southern states had merchants who made tokens with slogans calling for a united South. Northern states' slogans included "The Federal Union It Must and Shall Be Preserved."

There were even tokens produced by merchants known as sutlers. The sutlers were the official merchants of the United States Army and they formed a sort of traveling post exchange (PX). They would stock canned milk, meat, coffee, gift items, and numerous other commodities. Their minimum markup was from 300 per cent to 500 per cent over retail. Their goods were bought despite the high prices because they traveled with the troops, often in remote territories where there was no competition from city stores. Careful accounts were kept and money to pay the sutler was deducted from a soldier's paycheck before he received his money. Many a soldier reached payday only to find that he owed the sutler as much or more than he was to have received. Under such circumstances the soldier would leave the paymaster empty-handed.

The sutlers used both tokens and paper money as change when purchases were made for cash. Since the tokens and currency were only of value in that particular sutler's merchandise tent, they couldn't be spent elsewhere. Thus even when giving change, the sutler made certain he retained a captive group of buyers.

The general public was hostile to the use of tokens because of the difficulties they encountered. If the tokens issued by one store were offered to the proprietor of another store as payment for merchandise, they might or might not be accepted. If the issuing store had been in business for a while, was solvent, and was respected in the community, then the tokens could pass at face value. If the issuing store owner's reputation was not so good, the tokens would be rejected or downgraded everywhere else. People had to either use the tokens with the issuing merchant or lose a sum of money equal to the value of the tokens.

One answer to this problem was invented by a man named John Gault, and his solution is of interest to both coin and stamp collectors. He felt that the public needed a coin substitute that had a consistent, recognized value. Paper money was not yet being issued by the federal government, although states and banks had issued notes of various types over the years. However, the government was selling postage stamps, and everyone looked upon the small pieces of paper as having consistent value, just like gold and silver.

Gault used postage stamps as money, creating a holder for each stamp. The patent for Gault's invention was dated August 12, 1862. It was for a round metal case into which a postage stamp was inserted. Then a thin, almost transparent piece of mica was used to hold the stamp in place. The back of each holder had adequate space for an advertising message, making the item appealing to business people. The holder cost them money, of course, since the change given for merchandise was based on the face value of the stamp, not the cost of both the stamp and the case. But merchants felt they could better absorb the cost of the case than the loss of business due to a lack of small change.

Gault's business was short-lived. The merchants and general public delighted in what he was doing but the Post Office Department hated him. The Postmaster General complained that there were inadequate postage stamps to meet the needs of the mail. They couldn't also supply people buying stamps for use as small change. Gault was denied the large purchases he made at the start of his stamp-case manufacturing enterprise and could not meet the demand. His business folded even though it had the potential for making him a millionaire.

The government recognized that something had to be done to correct the coin shortage. Union leaders were impressed with Gault's stamp idea and decided to modify the concept of stamps as money. At the end of August 1862, the Secretary of the Treasury authorized the issuing of what became known as postage currency. Special stamps measuring 3⅜ by 2¾ inches were printed on heavy paper. There were denominations ranging from five cents to fifty cents, with several of these pieces of currency printed on a sheet. At first the postal currency was perforated for easy separation, but later the perforations were eliminated and the sheets had to be cut. Many

This is an example of the front and the back of an encased postage stamp. The stamp was held in place by a thin sheet of mica, and the reverse held an advertising message. In this case it reads "Ayer's Sarsaparilla to Purify the Blood."

people took several pieces and clipped them together into blocks whose total value was one dollar, for easy handling.

The postage currency was so named because of the designs used on the different issues. The five-cent note had the same portrait design of Thomas Jefferson that was found on the five-cent stamps. Likewise, the ten-cent postage currency had the same design as on the ten-cent stamps. The twenty-five-cent issue had five identical images of the five-cent stamp, and the fifty-cent issue had five identical ten-cent-stamp designs on it.

The trouble with the postage currency was that the Post Office Department officials were still involved in their printing. Modifications in the concept were urged, and the end result was what was known as fractional currency, which served throughout the war. These paper-money pieces were issued through the Treasury Department and valued at various amounts of less than a dollar. They did not bear postage-stamp images but served the same purpose as a small-change substitute.

A number of changes occurred with coins

before and after the Civil War. Three-cent silver coins were issued in 1851, a denomination supposed to be of use in postage transactions but so little desired that 1873 was the last year these coins were struck. Three-cent coins in nickel were issued in 1865 and were produced until 1889. They were also never very popular.

From 1854 through 1889, three-dollar gold pieces were issued, again to help the Post Office Department. The coin could be used to buy one hundred stamps, but few people ever did. Demand was slight and the quantity struck was always limited. These coins are among the most valuable regular-issue gold coins collected today due to the limited number produced.

A one-dollar gold coin was introduced in 1849 and was struck, with two major design changes, for the next fifty years. Unfortunately, the coin had to be tiny because of the small amount of gold equal in value to a dol-

These are examples of the early three-cent coins that were meant to ease the post-office change problem but never were popular. The one at left is a three-cent piece made in silver, which was introduced in 1851. The size is greatly en-

larged in the photograph, but the original was smaller than a dime. The one at right is larger than the three-cent silver piece and was a three-cent piece struck in nickel. It circulated from 1865 through 1889.

The three-dollar gold piece.

Gold dollars were among the smallest of American coins. This coin was much smaller than a dime and easily lost. Specimens of early gold dollars are quite popular with collectors, especially in uncirculated condition.

lar. People found they lost it easily and did not want to be bothered with it.

In 1856 a new type copper cent was introduced. This was a smaller coin than the large cent produced from the time the mint was founded. It had a rendering of a flying eagle on the obverse and was actually a "pattern," not a regular issue. The design was used only through 1858, and then an Indian-head obverse was utilized.

There is a popular but untrue story told about the creation of the Indian-head cent. The Indian is supposed to be modeled from the daughter of the designer, James Longacre. The small child, Sarah Longacre, was with her father at the mint the day some Indian chiefs were visiting. Supposedly one of the chiefs placed his headdress on the little girl's head and Longacre made a sketch from which the coin design evolved. In reality, though the incident with the chiefs may have occurred, the design was unrelated to his daughter, Sarah. The artist had been experimenting with this type of design for several years and had used it on some gold coins created when his daughter was either not yet born or a new infant

This gold-dollar variety was introduced in 1856 and was used until the coins ceased production in 1889.

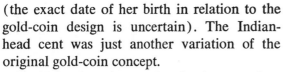

The Indian-head cent, one of the nation's most popular coins.

The two-cent piece was another of the coins that never quite caught the public fancy. Again stamps and taxes were considerations here, but no one was very interested.

(the exact date of her birth in relation to the gold-coin design is uncertain). The Indian-head cent was just another variation of the original gold-coin concept.

In 1864 the mint used a foreign metal to make a new coin. The metal was bronze, a popular European alloy of copper, tin, and zinc, and the coin was to be a two-cent piece.

The new two-cent piece has a special distinction in that it was the first coin to bear the motto "In God We Trust." The full story behind this motto is found in Chapter 5.

In 1873, a new type of silver dollar was introduced. This was a special coin of unusually high quality meant for use only in the Orient, where the Chinese demanded silver dollars in exchange for their goods. Previously the Chinese had relied almost exclusively on the Spanish dollars, which were reasonably consistent in the amount and quality of silver used in their manufacture during more than a century. However, the new United States trade dollars were carefully analyzed, then approved by Chinese bankers and merchants, who stamped Chinese letters into the coins. The re-

sults of this stamping are called "chop marks" and are extremely interesting. Since most collectors want the unmarked trade dollars, chop-marked coins are available at very low prices. Since the chop marks tell a story of international trade and the flawless coins may never have left this country, many collectors delight in seeing how many different symbols they can find on chop-marked coins. Such coins may never rise in value to any great degree but are fascinating to study.

Although American businessmen trading internationally had been seeking a silver coin they could use in the Orient, their needs were not really a major consideration when the coins were struck. The government authorized the new pieces primarily to appease the owners of silver mines, who had a very strong lobby in Congress. Regular silver dollars were in limited demand for domestic use, the West Coast being the only area where they were actively sought. As a result, from the end of 1873 until 1878, no regular-issue silver dollars were struck.

A chop-marked dollar. This was a Spanish eight-reales coin, which was used for trade in the Orient. These coins, as well as trade dollars from the United States and Great Britain, were all chop-marked to show that they were of proper intrinsic worth.

The trade dollar proved immensely popular in the Orient but unpopular in most of the United States. To make matters worse, the coins were declared to be legal tender in the United States only in amounts equal to a maximum of five dollars. All other silver coins were legal tender in any quantity, so this greatly reduced the coins' desirability in business.

By 1878, the trade-dollar demand had fallen so low that production of the coin was ordered stopped. The issues for 1879 through 1883 were what is known as proof coins. These are specially struck from highly polished dies and are sold to collectors rather than being released for circulation. Instead of 4¼ million coins being released in 1878 from the three mints of San Francisco, Carson City, and Philadelphia, just 1,541 proof coins were struck by Philadelphia alone in 1879. By 1883, the last official year of issue, less than 1,000 proof coins were struck.

Trade dollars were unofficially and illegally struck in 1884 and 1885, a situation that occasionally occurred before and after official strikings. Mint-originated coins not authorized by the United States Government were struck to make profits for mint workers in many cases. Dies may have existed for the 1884 coins—dies that should have been destroyed rather than used. However, no dies could legitimately have existed in 1885 due to changes in coin laws, and they were definitely fabricated for profit. Just ten 1884 and five 1885 copies of the trade dollar exist, and the 1885 coin is, today, one of the most expensive and highly prized American coins.

The first illegal U.S. coin was the 1804 silver dollar. Officially, silver-dollar production from new dies (a new die is needed each time the date changes) ended in 1803, and all the coins struck in 1804 were made from dies with earlier dates on them. During that period of history, it was common to never waste coin dies. If coins could be made from leftover dies dated earlier than the year of striking, they were. It was only after the old dies were used that new dies with the current date were prepared. In 1804, enough older dies existed so it was unnecessary to make current-dated dies, so all legal silver dollars for 1804 bear earlier dates.

Silver-dollar production ended in 1804 and was not resumed for circulation until 1840, although patterns and proofs were made for silver-dollar coins as early as 1836. Sometime around 1834, the mint was assembling a collection of coins to be used as presents for various foreign dignitaries. Silver dollars were to be included, and the mint director looked for the most recently struck dollars he could find. Nothing was available dated any later than 1803, though he noticed the mint records showed coins being struck in 1804. Since he didn't know that earlier-dated dies had been used, he assumed that 1804 dollars really existed. He thus had dies prepared for striking a handful of 1804 dollars to place in the presentation sets. These coins are so rare that they were among the first to sell to collectors for over one hundred thousand dollars. Yet they are not legal issues and were made many years after their dates imply.

Although today the United States Mint and its branches are security-conscious and the staff members are honest, this was not always the case. At one time a number of mint employees even went so far as to start a private business making medals for anyone who wanted them. They used mint equipment and personnel, doing the work during mint business hours.

Other mint employees over the years have struck proofs and special uncirculated coins of higher-than-normal quality known as presentation pieces. These were given to friends or sold for a profit, all actions taken against the laws regulating coinage operations.

Perhaps the most famous of the illegal issues is the 1913 Liberty-head nickel, which was one of the first coins whose collectors' value exceeded one hundred thousand dollars, and was also was the subject of an episode of a television show called "Hawaii 5-O." Briefly, the coin was the work of a dishonest mint employee with access to vaults where the dies for striking a 1913-dated nickel with Liberty-head design (see illustration) were kept. In 1913 James Earl Fraser had been commissioned to produce a new buffalo/Indian-head nickel. He was late in getting his design approved, and Liberty-head dies were made as a precautionary measure. They were only to be used if coins with the new Indian/buffalo design could not be struck in time to meet the 1913 coinage needs. However, the new nickel design was approved and the dies for the 1913 Liberty-head coins were destroyed. Before this could be done, though, the employee made five 1913 Liberty-head nickels using the genuine but abandoned dies and mint equipment. These coins were then hidden for several years.

When the mint employee had been retired

The Liberty-head nickel as originally introduced. Note the lack of the word "CENTS" on the reverse.

The corrected reverse for the Liberty-head nickels. The word "CENTS" had been added at the bottom.

The Saint-Gaudens twenty-dollar gold piece is considered the most beautiful coin ever struck in the United States. This is a later example when the relief was not so high as on the first year of issue. It could be easily prepared for coinage. However, even with the modifications, it remained a beautiful coin.

for a few years and decided it was safe, he began advertising that he would pay several hundred dollars for 1913-dated Liberty nickels. He advertised for many weeks in order to generate an interest, then announced that he had located five of the coins from an unnamed source. These were first sold to an eccentric multimillionaire collector named Colonel Edward Green. After Green's death, collectors bought single coins from the estate and, today, each of the five specimens is highly prized.

President Theodore Roosevelt was responsible for encouraging some of the United States' most beautiful coins. He was a lover of ancient Greek and Roman art, including the beautiful designs used on their coinage. He was determined to encourage artists unrelated to the mint employees, whom he felt lacked talent, to participate in coin design.

The first coin over which Roosevelt had strong influence was the twenty-dollar gold piece. He persuaded internationally famous sculptor Augustus Saint-Gaudens to design a classic-style coin. The beautiful figure of Liberty that graces the obverse is the result.

Saint-Gaudens also designed a ten-dollar gold piece that had a simpler design. It was a bust of Liberty wearing an Indian headdress. A similar concept, showing a male in the headdress, was placed on the five-dollar gold piece designed by Bela Pratt. The design of the five-dollar coin was stamped into the surface rather than raised above it, as was the case with other American coins.

The Lincoln cent was introduced in 1909 and was greatly appreciated by Roosevelt even though it wasn't a classical design. The coin also proved to be the most popular one ever issued by the U. S. Government. It was introduced at a time when the Ku Klux Klan was becoming increasingly powerful and influential in Congress. Minority groups were surprised when the coin was introduced, having assumed the political climate was hostile toward the man who freed the slaves. Most people figured the coin would be changed to honor someone less controversial. They thought that if they didn't get one or more of the cents on the day of issue, they would never get one. As a result, each distribution point for the new coins was swamped on the first day of issue. Near riots resulted in the lines of people that stretched for several blocks.

But the public fears were unfounded and the coin has circulated without major obverse design changes for approximately seventy years. It is also the first coin collected by many beginners in the hobby.

The Indian-head/buffalo nickel was introduced in 1913, as has been mentioned. Although this is often considered our best-known design and the one that most depicts the United States' history, the models were not typical of the Old West. Artist James Fraser used three different Indians as the models for the various features on his Indian-head nickel, and one of the three worked in a Coney Island

sideshow. The buffalo was Black Diamond, who lived in Central Park Zoo in New York City. Although Black Diamond gained international fame through the coin, he was eventually slaughtered for his meat and hide.

In 1916, three coins made their debut and all were based on Roosevelt's classic-coin preference. One was the Mercury dime with the head of Liberty looking much like Mercury, the mythological messenger of the gods. The model was Mrs. Wallace Stevens, wife of one of the nation's most famous poets. She and her husband were renting an apartment from Adolph Weinman, the artist who produced the coin, so she was close at hand.

Weinman also created the Walking-Liberty half dollar, which many people feel is our most beautiful mass-circulation coin. Weinman was a student of Saint-Gaudens, and the influence of the classical art is evident in both their creations.

The third coin, the Standing-Liberty quarter, was also the United States' only "obscene" coin. The designer, Hermon MacNeil, left

The buffalo nickel had to be modified in 1913 when it was introduced. The coin did not stack properly and it was necessary to lower the mound and make other changes. The reverse left was the first one used. The reverse right shows the modification.

The Mercury dime.

The Walking-Liberty half dollar designed by Adoph Weinman is considered America's most beautiful regular-issue coin. He was a student of Saint-Gaudens and had a small collection of copies of ancient coins, which he greatly admired.

Miss Liberty with a large exposure of thigh and one bare breast. The mint officials either didn't notice what he had done or didn't feel anyone would mind. The coin went into circulation, shocking millions who took a close look at the new design. As a result, midway through 1917, the second year of issue, the design was changed so that Miss Liberty's thigh was draped and her breast covered by armor. At no time, however, did the mint ever admit it made a mistake.

This is the notorious "obscene" Standing-Liberty quarter and the design change that was ordered. Note that the breast was covered with chain mail and the drape was lowered on her thigh. The reverse is shown below.

In recent years the coinage of the United States has honored its Presidents. The one exception was the Franklin half dollar (1948–1963), which honored the man considered to be one of our greatest Revolutionary War leaders, Benjamin Franklin.

Today we have a quarter honoring George Washington, a half dollar honoring John Kennedy, a dime honoring Franklin Roosevelt, a nickel honoring Thomas Jefferson, and a dollar coin honoring Dwight Eisenhower. The dime, quarter, half dollar, and dollar are all copper-nickel clad instead of silver, as in the past. Silver became so expensive that to use it in coinage after 1964 would have meant we would either have had to reduce the size of the coins or they would have an intrinsic worth greater than face value. At this writing, all silver coins issued by the United States in past years are worth approximately three times their face value in silver content alone.

The present coin designs, like those of earlier years, are protected by law. A design prepared for normal circulation must be produced for twenty-five years before it is changed. The only exception occurs when a special congressional act is passed, as was the case when the Kennedy half dollar was

The Franklin half dollar. The almost nonexistent eagle on the reverse was added when it was discovered one was necessary by law.

created after only sixteen years of the Franklin half-dollar design.

The only type of coin desired by collectors in large numbers and not previously mentioned are the commemorative coins. In 1893, a world's fair, the World's Columbian Exposition, was held in Chicago. The World's Columbian Exposition, honoring Columbus' discovery of America, was financed with a combination of federal funds, the sale of bonds, fees paid by exhibitors, and a series of commemorative coins. These included a quarter dollar honoring Queen Isabella, who financed Columbus' voyage to the New World, and a half dollar honoring Columbus.

The World's Columbian Exposition was a major international event. The world's most unusual ride, a giant wheel with seats for passengers, invented by a man named Ferris, was on the grounds. The top of the wheel was 265 feet above the ground and the wheel was 250 feet in diameter.

The exposition also honored scientific achievement. Electricity, only recently gaining wide use, was utilized everywhere. The fifteen buildings on the grounds were illuminated by five thousand arc lamps. There was also an exhibit of Thomas Edison's many inventions.

The exposition even had a touch of "sinfulness." The "notorious" Little Egypt did her belly dance while keeping her midriff exposed, a sensuous delight that shocked the public.

The coins sold to help pay for the fair were authorized under a special act of Congress. They were all legal tender and remain so today. However, they were sold specifically as souvenirs and collectors' items at double the face value.

In the years that followed, other groups sponsoring events were allowed to sell commemorative half dollars honoring the celebration and struck by the U. S. Mint. Each time, the coins sold for double the face value and were legal tender.

There were a few exceptions among the commemorative issues. In 1900, a dollar coin was struck in silver to honor the Lafayette Memorial. Gold dollars were struck honoring the Louisiana Purchase (1903), the Lewis and Clark voyages (1904), the Panama Pacific Exposition (1915), the McKinley Memorial (1916 and 1917), and the Grant Memorial (1922). In addition, the Panama

When is a Jefferson nickel not a nickel? When it is made from silver. In 1942 through 1945, most of the Jefferson five-cent pieces were made from

silver since nickel was essential for wartime uses. The silver coins are identifiable by the mint mark visible directly over the top of Monticello.

Pacific Exposition of 1915 saw commemorative quarter eagles and both round and octagonal $50 gold pieces. Another $2.50 commemorative gold piece was struck in 1926.

The series of commemorative half dollars and other coins first struck in 1892 came to an end in 1954. The last half dollars, just under 150,000 from the three mints (Denver, San Francisco, and Philadelphia), were struck that year in honor of Booker T. Washington and George Washington Carver.

During America's Bicentennial in 1976, new reverse designs were added to the Kennedy half dollar, Eisenhower dollar, and Washington quarter. These were determined by a contest open to every artist in the nation. The designs were used for 1976 only, and the obverse had a special 1776–1976 date. Because the designs were used just one year, these coins are also considered to be commemorative issues, though in use for regular coinage.

As you can see, there is a tremendous variety of coins available to the collector of United States issues. This is why they have always proven popular over the years. But other countries have equally interesting coins, as will be seen in following chapters.

Chapter 3

CANADIAN AND MEXICAN COINAGE

When an American collector first decides to branch into coins of other countries, chances are he or she will look to those areas touching our borders. The histories of Mexico and Canada are so intertwined with our own that collecting of the beautiful and often unusual forms of specie produced throughout the world.

Canada's earliest monetary system was a conglomeration of Indian currency, barter items, and coins carried in the pockets of European explorers. Wampum served as money for both Indians and whites, as did beaver skins and necessities such as wheat. White traders dealing with the Northwest Coast Indians discussed that blankets and giant copper plates represented the extremes of wealth. Blankets were owned by even the poorest, and it took five hundred blankets to buy a slave. Copper plates, on the other hand, were relatively rare, and their possession brought great pride of ownership. Ten slaves or five thousand blankets was the usual cost of just one of these plates. They were so admired that they were given names meant to show their value.

One such name, for example, was "All Other Coppers Are Ashamed to Look at It."

As settlements evolved, Canada was split into two parts. One section was French territory and the other was British. Both had coinage needs, but the French proved the more ingenious in easing the small-change shortage. They made their own money—out of playing cards.

The early French colonists in Canada were left on their own by the King. Although their permanent settlements required a supply of money, the people were shipped very little and were forbidden to manufacture their own coins. Merchants and traders brought some coins to the colonists, but such men usually ended by taking even more back to Europe in payment for the many goods the colonists imported.

At first the colonial leaders tried to solve the problem by overvaluing the coins that were in circulation. The coins were worth one third more than their face value in trade. Unfortunately, instead of easing the coin shortage, this approach only resulted in the people

33

having to spend more of their money when they ordered goods from abroad.

Perhaps the most difficult problem was paying for the troops who were on temporary duty in the colonies. These men would be returning to France after their tour of duty in Canada, and they insisted on receiving coins they could spend when they returned.

The problem reached critical proportions in 1685. The people of the colony were trying to make do with barter, beaver skins, and anything else of value. However, the colonial leaders had to have coins for the soldiers. Jacques de Meulles, the leader of the colony who held the rather pompous title of "Chevalier Councellor to the King in Councils, Seigneur de la Source, Grand Bailly d'Orleans, Intendant of Justice, Police, and Finance," found himself using his own wealth to pay the troops. Then one day de Meulles had an ingenious idea for supplying funds.

The French Government was sending a shipment of coins to the French colonies every year. Most of these shipments arrived safely. A number were lost at sea. De Meulles knew that he would always be reimbursed for whatever method he used to pay the troops, but that did not make the problem any easier.

At first, de Meulles tried issuing the troops promissory notes detailing how much they would be paid. This had been done in the past and was reasonably acceptable to the men. But just a scrawled promise to pay did not seem adequate.

One day de Meulles noticed the men playing cards, a pastime that had been popular with Frenchmen since 1361. Every soldier had one or more packs of playing cards he took with him everywhere. The cards, blank on one side, were used for all manner of games and were in great abundance in the colony. De Meulles decided to use the cards in order to produce a form of paper money. He later wrote the leaders of the French Government concerning what he had done. One September 24, 1685, he wrote, in part:

". . . I find myself in great straits regarding the sustenance of the soldiers; you have not ordered the funds; now, My Lord, from January until September, eight whole months, I have not ceased from my efforts to furnish them with sufficient to keep them alive. I have drawn from my own chest and from those of my friends all that I could, but at length seeing them in such a plight without power to render them proper service and not knowing to what saint to make my vow, money being extremely scarce having been distributed at all costs in considerable sums for the payment of the soldiers, the idea occurred to me of putting into circulation in place of money card notes, which I caused to be cut in four; I send you, My Lord, a sample of the three values, one is four francs, another forty sols, and the third fifteen sols, because with these values I can make the right change for a soldier's monthly pay. I used an ordinance commanding the people to accept this money when tendered and to give it currency, at the same time obliging myself to redeem the said notes; no one refused them, which had such a good effect that the troops have been able to subsist as usual."

The use of playing cards as money proved extremely popular. These were specially marked and signed by de Meulles and by his successors, who also used the idea during the shortage of coins. Whenever the ship would arrive with money from France, de Meulles would call in the specially altered cards and exchange them for legal coins.

The cards were issued periodically over the years, eventually becoming acceptable as money on their own. More cards were issued than there was coinage to back them, and inflation became a problem. Merchants demanded far more cards than their equivalent worth in coinage, effectively raising prices for those who used them. Nevertheless, they continued to be used into the late 1700s. By then the British were entrenched in Canada, controlling all the land once held by the French, and the use of the cards was declared illegal.

Collectors of Canadian coins highly prize the few playing-card money pieces still to be found. Bids in excess of one thousand dollars are not unusual when an occasional card finds its way to auction.

The first coins that could be called Canadian were struck in 1670. French King Louis XIV authorized two silver coins and a copper coin to be designed and struck specifically for use in Canada. Prior to that time, the French colonists had to make do with the legal-tender pieces normally circulating in Europe.

The silver pieces, fifteen sols and five sols in denomination, showed the King's portrait on the obverse and the French coat of arms on the reverse. While no direct equivalent can be made, they might be compared to the dime and quarter. The inscription in Latin translated to mean "They Shall Speak of the Glory of Thy Kingdom." The copper coin that was authorized is almost unknown and probably never reached Canada. Thus the people were denied small change and had to rely on a copper/silver-alloy (*billion* was the name of the metal) coin called a *mousquetaire*. They were issued for four years starting in 1709, and many were imported into Canada.

In 1721, the French Government finally got around to producing a Canadian copper coin about the size and value of the American large cent described in the previous chapter. Great quantities of these small coins were shipped to Quebec. However, the *mousquetaires* were so numerous and so popular that no one wanted the new coins. The majority of them were stored, unused, in a warehouse, where they remained for many years. Finally most of them were returned to France for melting.

Between 1719 and 1721, French Canada had gold, silver, and copper coins struck for its use through the instigation of a man named John Law. John Law was an unusual French official in that he was born and raised in Scotland. He moved to France, however, became friendly with King Louis, and worked himself into the position of being the King's financial adviser. He was convinced that the Canadian colony would be able to find and exploit vast mineral wealth that would bring riches to France. He had the King issue paper money and stock certificates that would be redeemed with this money. He also arranged for the coins that had denominations in gold of a twenty-*livre* Louis d'Or and a demi or half Louis d'Or. The silver coins were valued at twenty sols and ten sols, while the copper coins were valued at six deniers and three deniers. Unfortunately, though Law's intentions were good, the coins were never adequate to meet colonial needs.

The British Government had settlements in Lower Canada that were at odds with the French holdings. Britain was involved in expansionist activities in all of North America, leading to bitter rivalries with the French and, eventually, to war. This was actually an extension of the war already being waged in Europe by the two countries. By 1763, England controlled all of the territories once known as New France. The Canadian territory was divided into two parts, the French-speaking Upper Canada and the English-speaking Lower Canada, both under British control. It was not until 1867, after the Canadian people violently agitated for a more independent form of government, that the upper and lower territories were combined and given the right to internal self-government.

The British colonies had the same coin-shortage problems as those of France, but their methods for handling the difficulty were somewhat different. Prince Edward Island, for example, had difficulty obtaining English coins but found that the Spanish milled dollar or eight-reales coin was fairly common. Unfortunately, since the Spanish coins were acceptable throughout the world, most of them were constantly being shipped abroad to pay for imported goods.

The leaders of the island's settlers decided to ease the coin shortage and keep the Spanish money in circulation by cleverly defacing the

A holey dollar made from a Spanish eight-reales coin and circulated in Canada. It is identical to the concept used in Australia.

At first these "holey dollars" (the doughnut pieces) and "dumps" (centers), as they were called, circulated widely. The people liked the concept and willingly accepted them. However, it was soon learned that the size of the dumps meant that they contained more than a shilling's worth of silver. The people found that they could make a substantial profit by accumulating the dumps, then shipping them back to England for melting. The price they received for the silver not only offset the cost of accumulating and shipping the dumps, it also gave them a substantial profit. As a result, while holey dollars remained reasonably available, dumps became quite scarce.

There is some argument among experts as to whether or not the surviving holey dollars and dumps are the original coins issued by the island leaders. Numerous counterfeits were introduced over the years, since anyone could remove the center of the Spanish coins. The island leaders had wanted to limit the number of holey dollars and dumps in circulation, but many additional pieces were introduced. The merchants were delighted, however, and readily accepted all the coins. Whether or not the examples remaining are originals or counterfeits is the subject of debate.

During the early 1800s, tokens were imported from England to serve as small change. A large variety of these tokens exist, and variations of this concept continued to circulate in Canada for well over a hundred years. Some of the early tokens contain an Irish harp on the obverse and a reverse reading SHIPS COLONIES & COMMERCE.

The early tokens generally were valued at a halfpenny or one sou, depending upon whether they were originally to circulate in a French-speaking section such as Quebec or in the English-speaking areas. One showed a ship and had the slogan FOR PUBLIC ACCOMODATION. Others, issued by companies, bore such advertising slogans as CASH PAID FOR ALL TYPES OF GLASS and J. SHAW & CO. IMPORTERS OF

coins. A hole was punched from the center of each coin. This left the people with a doughnut-shaped outer section, which was officially valued at five shillings, and a small, circular piece, the center of the coin, which was valued at one shilling. The total amount, six shillings, was more than the value of the Spanish dollar undefaced.

HARDWARES UPPER TOWN QUEBEC. The reverses bore designs ranging from saws, shovels, and other hardware to a beer barrel to examples of glasswork.

The tokens were as acceptable to merchants and the general public as coins would have been. In fact, at least one counterfeiter is known to have made the tokens because he felt they were as valuable as coins. He worked for Joseph Roy, a token manufacturer, in the late 1830s and counterfeited tokens in order to buy beer he could not afford on his salary. Rather than press charges or raise the employee's salary, Roy redeemed all the tokens, legitimate or otherwise.

Tokens were also issued for use when trading with the Indians and Eskimos. This practice started with the North West Company, which was founded in Montreal in 1784 and began issuing tokens valued at one beaver pelt as early as 1820. The Hudson's Bay Company followed suit in 1857, taking the concept one step farther. Tokens were issued for a whole beaver skin, a half, a quarter, and an eighth skin. The individual skins were so valuable that the most commonly traded token used by personnel in forts and other outposts was the one valued at an eighth of a beaver skin.

Numerous varieties of brass and, after World War II, aluminum tokens have been used by the Hudson's Bay Company. Some were in multiples of twenty cents. Others bore standard coin values of one cent, and five, ten, twenty-five, fifty and one hundred cents. There were also sticks, laid out in rows, with each stick equaling an animal skin worth fifty cents. If an animal skin was more valuable, several sticks were used. Thus an Eskimo bringing in a silver-fox skin might get thirty such sticks rather than one.

The sticks and tokens were not money. Rather they were counters used to keep track of purchases. The Eskimos would enter the trading post with their skins and the proprietor would lay the appropriate number of tokens, sticks, or other objects (buttons, thim-

bles, and similarly odd devices were used in some areas) on the counter. Then the Eskimos would select the goods they needed, the proprietor removing whatever tokens were of equal value. Generally all the tokens were used at the time of the exchange rather than being carried off by the Eskimos. They were not coins and had no value from Eskimo to Eskimo. Rather, they were more like a bookkeeping device.

The most numerous tokens were what might be considered semi-official "coins" since they were issued by a Canadian financial institution. The Bank of Montreal began striking copper tokens in 1835, a year when most of the merchants' tokens were declared illegal. These new tokens featured the design of a bouquet of flowers and were valued according to French money at *un sous*.

Two years later, a similar token was issued by the Banque de Peuple. It was followed by imitation Bank of Montreal tokens struck in bronze and popular with rebellious citizens hostile to the British, who dominated the for-

A bank token of Canada; this one circulated in 1837.

merly French territory. More than forty varieties of these imitations were struck.

The Bank of Montreal continued to strike tokens despite the imitations. Some were val-

A halfpenny token.

Many of the banks issued tokens using the St. George and the dragon symbolism of the mother country, England.

ued at a penny or a halfpenny. Others followed the earlier concept. The designs changed over the years, perhaps to foil the imitators, and the pieces were a mainstay of the community's business transactions.

The Province of Canada, formed in 1858, adopted the decimal system, and England finally began issuing a series of coins for Canadian use. These coins were in denominations of one cent, and five, ten, and twenty cents. They featured the head of Queen Victoria with a laurel wreath in her hair.

Nova Scotia and New Brunswick were treated independently and did not get their first coins until after they adopted the decimal system in 1860. Nova Scotia was sent half cents and cents in 1861, with similar denominations for New Brunswick. However, New Brunswick's needs were considered to be greater, and the people were also sent five-, ten-, and twenty-cent pieces during the next three years.

The year 1867 saw the creation of the Dominion of Canada, which combined New Brunswick, the Province of Canada, and Nova Scotia. Six years later, Prince Edward Island became a part of the united country.

England continued to be the source of coins for the new Dominion. Five-cent, ten-cent, twenty-five-cent, and fifty-cent pieces were struck in 1870, the coins bearing the youthful head of Queen Victoria. She is surrounded by the motto "VICTORIA DEI GRATIA REGINA CANADA."

There is a sameness about the early years of Canada's coinage. Each succeeding monarch appeared with a relatively unchanging design. The main difference in the coins is that the head of the ruler is turned in the opposite direction of his or her predecessor. Victoria faced to the left, Edward VII is shown facing right, George V faced left, and so forth. The only apparent break in the pattern resulted when Edward VIII abdicated the throne, after serving only briefly, to marry a commoner. Since he would have been facing right on the coins, by tradition, George VI, his successor, is shown facing left. However, since no coins were actually issued for Edward VIII, two succeeding issues have the monarch facing in the same direction.

A humorous aspect of Edward VIII's brief reign came when he wanted to defy the tradition of having his coin portrait face the opposite way from his royal predecessor. His right profile should have appeared on the coinage, but he felt that his left side was far better looking than his right. He refused to allow his right profile to be shown. Even offers to have an artist transfer his image so the features of his right side would be seen on the left for the coin did not end his determination to defy tradition. The mint director was quite relieved when Edward abdicated, and the mint did not have to produce a coin that would have altered the tradition.

In 1901, the population of Canada had reached such numbers that shipping coins from England was no longer practical. The decision was made to establish a branch mint for Canada, to be located in Ottawa. After four years of planning, construction was started, with completion in 1908. Eventually the nation gained two more mints, one in Hull, Quebec, and the other in Winnipeg, Manitoba.

In 1910, the decision was made to create a silver dollar for Canada. The coin, containing the portrait of George V on the obverse, was struck as a test. Three have been discovered at this writing, though there may be one or two more. At least one specimen is in lead. The coin, considered the greatest rarity among all Canadian issues, has sold for a high of $135,000 at this writing and its potential value can only be guessed.

Far more affordable for the average collector is the first silver dollar to go into general circulation. This was issued in 1935 and was meant to commemorate the twenty-fifth anniversary of George V's ascension to the throne.

With this first silver dollar for general circu-

lation, the Canadian Government established a tradition that makes Canada's silver dollars immensely popular with collectors in many countries. The coin was a commemorative with a reverse design that was unusual for North American mint products. The obverse was a simple portrait bust of the King. But the reverse had the Northern Lights radiating across an island. In the water is a canoe being paddled by a *voyageur,* the name given to the early Canadian explorers, and an Indian. It proved so popular that the Royal Canadian Mint reported, in 1935:

"There was a steady demand for these coins from the first issue in May until the end of the year, when their coinage was discontinued, and it is considered that a large number of them have been placed in collections or have been retained as souvenirs, and are not likely, for some years at least, to form part of the general circulation."

This speculation proved true. While there were less than a half million struck, the Canadian coin remains relatively inexpensive in uncirculated condition. A less popular United States coin of somewhat less scarcity, the 1938 Walking-Liberty half dollar produced by the Denver Mint, sells for ten times the uncirculated price of the first *voyageur* dollar. This is because the 1938-D half went almost entirely into circulation.

In 1939, under King George VI, Canada redesigned the reverse of the silver dollar to show a building complex—the Peace Tower of Ottawa's Parliament Building and the Center Block. It was meant to commemorate the visit of King George VI and Queen Elizabeth to Canada in May and June of that year.

Silver dollars stopped being made during World War II. Such coins circulated less than others, could be duplicated with paper money, and were unnecessary for normal change. Thus they were a luxury the country could not afford until peace came in 1945. The new dollars retained the *voyageur* reverse.

Four years later, in 1949, the dollar was

Canadian silver dollars. These show some of the many commemorative approaches to design that have made Canadian silver dollars so popular among collectors.

redesigned to honor Newfoundland's entry into the Confederation of Canada. The reverse shows an intricately engraved sailing ship, the *Mathew,* which was used by John Cabot when he discovered Newfoundland in 1497. Directly below the vessel are the words "FLOREAT TERRA NOVA," which translated to "May the new-found land flourish."

The 1958 dollar, with Elizabeth II on the obverse, commemorated the hundredth anniversary of the gold rush and the creation of British Columbia as a Crown Colony. The coin features a totem pole on the reverse and has been called Canada's ugliest dollar. This is subject to debate, for it represents one of the most unusual aspects of native culture in that region.

Totem poles were carved by the western Indians as honors for a select group of men. The figures were all symbolic of events in the lives of the man and his family. The carving was done by a limited number of artists who traveled the countryside practicing their trade.

Totem poles were raised with great celebration. Often the men considered qualified to have totem poles were also wealthy. They kept numerous slaves, the ultimate symbol of wealth. When they attended a pole-raising ceremony for someone else, they liked to show their wealth by clubbing to death several of their slaves, then tossing the bodies into the deep pit where the totem pole eventually would be erected. This was the equivalent of a more civilized man showing his wealth by lighting a cigar with a hundred-dollar bill.

The 1964 Canadian silver dollar is perhaps the least interesting design among the commemorative issues. It commemorated the 1864 Conferences of the Fathers of Confederation, which preceded by three years the actual establishment of the Confederation of Canada. The reverse is best described by the 1964 mint report, which stated in part:

"The design of the reverse impression to depict, conjoined within a circle, the French *fleur-de-lis,* the Irish shamrock, the Scottish thistle, and the English rose surrounded by the names 'CHARLOTTETOWN' and 'QUEBEC'; the whole enclosed by the words 'CANADA' above, 'DOLLAR' below, and the figures '1864' at the left and '1964' at the right, together with a graining upon the edge of the coin."

Three years later, the dollar design commemorated the Centennial of the Confederation of Canada. A simpler design was chosen consisting of a Canadian goose in flight.

In 1970, the silver dollar showed a magnificent prairie crocus when it honored the hundredth anniversary of Manitoba's entry into the Dominion of Canada. A flower, or, more precisely, two dogwood blossoms, were used for the 1971 dollar commemorating British Columbia's link with the Confederation. The blossoms are shown over the British Columbia coat of arms.

Architecture returned to the dollar in 1973. This time the structure shown was less elaborate than during the royal visit several years earlier. The coin commemorated the link of Prince Edward Island with the Dominion of Canada a hundred years earlier. The design featured the Prince Edward Island Provincial Legislature Building.

Perhaps the most complex dollar Canada has ever issued was struck in 1974. Winnipeg, Manitoba, celebrated its first century as a Canadian city. A large numeral 100 is on the reverse, each "0" in the 100 containing a street scene. The first "0" shows Winnipeg as it looked one hundred years earlier. There are low-rise buildings, a chimney billowing thick smoke, and an oxcart being driven down the street. The second "0" shows the same location, this time with modern high-rise buildings and automobiles jamming the street.

The silver and, after 1968, nickel dollars may have the most dramatic designs of Canada's coins, but the small change saw a number of variations over the years as well. In 1942, for example, nickel was in short supply and it became necessary to use an alloy known as tombac for the five-cent pieces. This alloy consisted of 88 per cent copper and 12 per cent zinc. To underscore the difference in the coin, it was made in the shapt of an octagon rather than being circular. By 1946, nickel was again in use, but the five-cent pieces remained multisided. Only in 1963 were the nickels again made round.

From 1937, when the first George VI issue was released, until 1966, the beaver graced Canada's nickels. In 1967, to commemorate the Centennial, a rabbit became the main

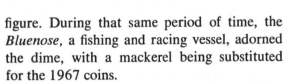

Some general coinage of Canada.

a half-dollar series starting in 1937. The design was changed in 1959 when Canada developed a new coat of arms. The earlier version showed the Imperial Crown mounted on top of a shield. A lion, a harp, a rampant lion, and three *fleur-de-lis* symbolized England, Ireland, Scotland, and France, respectively. On the right is a unicorn with a lance bearing the flag of Royalist France. On the left is a rampant lion holding the Union Jack. A stem of maple leaves at the bottom completes the design.

The revised coat of arms is more dramatic in appearance. A lion holding a maple leaf sits atop a spade-shaped shield. A unicorn holds a *fleur-de-lis* flag on the right and a lion holds a Union Jack on the left. There are heraldic flowers below the ribbon, and the various emblems within the shield found on the earlier coat of arms have been retained at reduced size. The slogan "A MARI USQUE AD MARE" (from sea to sea) was added at the bottom. During the Centennial, a howling wolf was used as a substitute for the coat of arms.

figure. During that same period of time, the *Bluenose,* a fishing and racing vessel, adorned the dime, with a mackerel being substituted for the 1967 coins.

The quarter-dollar series used a caribou reverse when George VI was on the throne. This continued until the Centennial year, when the reverse showed a wildcat.

The Canadian coat of arms was utilized for

42

The cent had the least interesting design, as perhaps befits the lowliest of coins. A maple leaf sufficed over the years, with a dove taking its place for the 1967 issue.

Canada has had a series of gold coins during its history. From 1908 through 1919 the country produced gold pieces known as sovereigns, a denomination that did not relate to the decimal system of coinage used by Canada. The coins were meant for use during trade with the other British Commonwealth countries, the majority of which used the pound sterling system, which included the sovereign denomination.

From 1912 through 1914, Canada also issued gold five- and ten-dollar coins for domestic use. These were never very popular, as the short production period indicates. The design for the coins was a variation of the coat of arms, while the sovereign used a symbol popular with the British. It showed a mounted St. George slaying the dragon.

A twenty-dollar gold piece was also made but it was a special commemorative for 1967, not a coin meant for circulation. It was available in sets alone with the copper and silver coins. These sets were frequently smuggled into the United States during the period when U.S. citizens could not legally import or own gold coins of contemporary mintage.

The 1967 gold coin started a precedent for the Canadian mints. It was decided that each year coins would be made available to collectors which, while theoretically legal tender, were not expected to circulate. These were sold at a premium and made from silver instead of nickel. They were unusually well struck with surfaces that are similar to the American proof coins, which are specially prepared from highly polished dies and sold for a considerable amount over face value.

In 1971, the special collector's dollar honoring British Columbia had the standard portrait obverse featuring Queen Elizabeth II. The reverse features a heraldic design known as the Ensigns Armorial of British Columbia.

The 1972 dollar has the *voyageur* reverse familiar from the regular issues. However, the coin was made from silver rather than nickel.

The 1973 collector issue features a member of the Royal Canadian Mounted Police. The coin is remarkable in its detail, the weapons and saddle parts clearly visible with a magnifying glass.

In 1974, the collector dollar was the same Winnipeg commemorative issued for general circulation. The only difference is that this coin is half silver and half copper rather than being made from nickel.

One of the "liveliest" collector dollar designs was issued in 1975. It honored Calgary, Alberta, in the Canadian "Wild West." A cowboy is shown astride a bucking bronco with the modern city seen at a distance on the left side and oil wells visible on the right.

The collector dollar for 1976 shows an architectural design. This time the Library of Parliament is shown on the collector coin, honoring the library's hundredth anniversary.

The Silver Jubilee of Queen Elizabeth II's ascension to the throne of the United Kingdom was celebrated in 1977. The collector dollar shows her Throne of the Senate in front of a wall of blocks. It is the throne used during ceremonial occasions, and the design is perhaps the least attractive in this series.

The 1978 collector dollar is an extremely unusual design meant to honor the Eleventh Commonwealth Games in Edmonton. The reverse is divided into blocks, which show the ten different symbols representing the various events. These include everything from track events to weight lifting, bicycle riding, and riflery. The obverse has the standard royal portrait but, for the first time on any Canadian coin, it also features the denomination.

One last series of coins must be mentioned before leaving Canada. These are the seven series of five- and ten-dollar coins and the hundred-dollar gold coins issued for the 1976 Olympic Games. When Canada learned that it would host the 1976 Olympics, government officials recognized that the cost would be enormous. There were no existing facilities large enough to hold the events, house the athletes, and handle the crowds. Millions of dollars would be needed, and the money had to come as much from the public as possible without adding a tax burden. The solution, which was partially successful, was to create a series of special Olympic coins to be sold to collectors. These were both uncirculated, the way a coin normally comes from the mint, and proof, specially struck from highly polished dies. The coins were issued between 1973 and 1976, the proof coins selling for considerably more money than the uncirculated specimens.

Briefly, the coins were issued in seven parts. The first coins featured geographic locations such as a map of North America; the skyline of Montreal, where the games were to be held; and similar points of interest. Four coins were issued with a face value of thirty dollars.

Series II again consisted of four coins, this time showing images symbolizing the Olympics. For example, an athlete with a torch is shown on one of the coins, and Zeus, the father of the Greek gods in whose honor the games were played, is shown on another.

The third series of four coins show some of the earliest sports popular in Canada. A game of lacrosse is being played by Indians on one coin, and bicyclists of the 1870s are shown on another.

The fourth series was dedicated to men's and women's track and field events, while the fifth issue honored water sports. The sixth series honored team activities, and the seventh showed the various buildings that would house the Olympic events. A total of twenty-eight different coins were issued in silver.

The gold coins issued in 1976 for collector purchase bore face values of one hundred dollars each. One coin was made from fourteen-carat gold, which means that almost half the coin was an alloy. The other was made from twenty-two-carat—almost pure—gold. Both coins show Elizabeth II's head on the obverse.

The identical reverses show the goddess Athena standing with one hand on the shoulder of an athlete who carries symbols indicating he has just won an athletic competition.

The gold coins proved popular enough with collectors that the mint felt there would be a demand for a similar gold commemorative the following year during Elizabeth II's Silver Jubilee. The reverse of this coin depicts all the flowers symbolizing Canada's territories and provinces. The obverse legend, near the portrait of the Queen, reads: "SILVER JUBILEE—ELIZABETH II 1952–1977—25 ANS DE REGNE."

While the Canadian coins, especially the silver and nickel dollars, have some of the most interesting commemorative designs in existence, Mexican coins are also popular with Americans. These were the first widely available coins in the British colonies, and they were intimately involved with our trade and commerce almost to the nineteenth century. The trade dollar of the 1870s and early 1880s was created, in part, to compete with some of the eight-reales coins from Mexico.

The last time you had a cup of hot cocoa or nibbled on a chocolate bar, you probably didn't feel particularly special. It only cost a few cents and it was the kind of snack you have with some degree of frequency. But if you had lived in Mexico several centuries ago, eating the chocolate would have been the equivalent of abandoning your new car the moment the gas tank was empty. Cacao beans, the fruit of the Mexican cacautal plant, was both a food—chocolate—and money for the people of the ancient Aztec Empire.

Money, as was mentioned earlier, has not always meant coins. People have often valued those goods that were needed for survival, sustenance, or daily living. Thus the cacao beans were valued as money precisely because they served as food. As a result, all goods and services were valued in terms of quantities of the beans.

The exact value of each bean was not recorded before the Spanish explorers conquered the Aztec civilization, though it is known that the largest value in the normal monetary transactions involved sacks of beans, each of which contained 24,000 cacao beans.

In 1611, Fernandez de Oviedo attempted to identify some of the items that could be purchased for fixed quantities of the cacao beans. He wrote, in part, in the *Historia Eclesiastica de Nuestro Tiempos:* "There is nothing among the natives that cannot be bought or sold with or for these nuts, just as among Christians with gold doubloons or double ducats. Thus a rabbit could be procured for 10 cacao beans; 2 zapotes [an apple-shaped fruit common to one of the native plants] were worth 1 cacao bean; a slave could be purchased for 100 cacao beans, and a concubine could be engaged for 8 or 10 beans."

The Spanish adopted the bean money in addition to their own coinage. They took their familiar coin value, the real, and designated that it was equivalent to 140 cacao beans. It is interesting to note that in remote areas of Mexico the beans still circulate today, with an average value of 40 beans being set for the smallest-denomination silver coins available in those areas.

It might seem that the cacao bean was the ideal form of money because it could not be counterfeited. After all, anyone can form silver into coins, but the cacao bean must be found in nature.

The immunity from counterfeiting was a false hope. The beans actually functioned on two levels—commerce and food. The beans that were used in commerce were almost never eaten, even though there was no difference between them and the ones that were consumed. The only check that was made concerning the bean used for trade was that it looked and felt normal. As a result, some men decided to have their wealth and eat it, too. They used an extremely sharp knife to carefully slit the bean, removing the sweet filling for food.

Then they would carefully fill the space inside the shell with dirt and press it together so the slit would not be noticed easily. The dirt-filled cacao shell had a weight and outer appearance similar to that of the normal bean.

The Spanish conquerers used different forms of cacao-bean money to establish a trade system satisfactory to both natives and conquerers alike. The Aztecs were conquered in bloody fighting during 1519–20. From that period until 1527, the cacao beans were counted individually for each purchase. However, the process was so time-consuming that measures of beans were authorized to be taken instead of the laborious counting. After 1527, different quantities were scooped from bags of the beans in order to pay for purchases. It was a less precise measure compared with the counting of individual beans but far more practical.

In 1555, beans were again counted individually for transactions. They had been fixed in value to an exact ratio of 140 beans to the real, and scooping the beans was not precise enough.

There were other types of primitive money used by the Aztecs. One type was made from copper, though its exact use is debatable. Some people think the copper pieces were used only for major transactions where counting the beans would have been impractical. This maintains that the copper pieces were used exclusively for commerce.

An alternative theory, which seems more likely, is that the copper pieces served as both money and working tools. The shape is a little like the head of a small hoe. The copper could have been used for scraping animal hides or working with pottery. Since the cacao bean served as both food and money, it seems logical that larger-denomination coppers would also have a function other than just being symbolic of wealth.

There were numerous other coin substitutes in use about the time the Spanish conquered the Aztecs and recorded the Mexican people's approach to commerce. Duck quills were filled with gold and sealed at the opening. The amount of dust was visible through the wall of the quill, and this allowed for reasonably consistent measures. Beads, shells, and even pieces of tin were also popular.

The Spanish conquerers were overwhelmed by the amount of gold they thought they had found in Mexico. Gold jewelry and ornamentation abounded, giving the impression that the land was rich in the precious metal. In reality, the people had very little gold. What seemed like a large amount was actually the total wealth the people had accumulated over the centuries. When the gold jewelry and implements readily visible were gone, there would be little, if any, to take their place. The land was not rich in underground gold deposits as the Spanish hoped.

What Mexico did have in abundance was silver. It was this silver that eventually convinced the Spanish Government that the conquest had not been in vain. However, at first, the conquerers were only interested in the more obvious gold as well as in exploiting the natives for cheap labor.

At first the Spanish conquerers utilized the gold for money and for sending to Spain. Gold that was not used in Aztec ornamentation was kept in the form of dust. The Spaniards found the shipping of dust too cumbersome. They began melting the gold, forming it into disks, and stamping them with the measured weight. The disks were so popular among the natives that many of the Spanish decided to cheat the people by mixing the gold in the disks with enough copper to debase them without adding so much that the color was altered.

It took approximately ten years for the Spanish conquerers of the Aztecs to find the true extent of the Mexican mineral wealth and to organize a system for taking full advantage of these riches. Most of the gold was exhausted, but the seemingly endless supply of silver had been uncovered and was being exported on a regular basis.

The Spanish Government had a rule that one fifth of all the precious metal taken from Spanish-controlled territory had to be sent to the royal treasury. This was extremely difficult when the metal was in the form of bullion, as the conquerers of Mexico quickly learned. An effort was made to allow a mint to be built so that the coins could be made from the silver, then divided so the Spanish Government got its share. This authorization came in 1535 with an order from King Charles I of Spain. Charles I was better known as Holy Roman Emperor Charles V.

All silver brought to the new mint, located in Mexico City, had to be marked to indicate that the royal fifth had been paid. From that fifth, the Spanish conquerers were authorized to withhold five hundred pounds of silver to pay for the cost of mint construction. The mint workers were also authorized to withhold three reales from every sixty-eight reales coined as payment for operating expenses.

The new mint, which began operating in 1536, was authorized to produce copper coins rated at four and two maravedis, the smallest denomination normally needed for business, and silver coins in denominations of one fourth, one half and one real, and two and three reales. However, while the natives recognized the value of silver and were accustomed to using it in their transactions, they did not recognize the value of copper coinage. They refused to use the small copper pieces in trade, and the mint was forced to concentrate on the silver issues.

The most important coin to come from the Mexican Mint was the eight-reales coin, the famous piece of eight of pirate lore. But the eight-reales denomination was more than thirty-five years in coming. It was not produced until 1572, many years after the major silver strike was made in the area known as Potosi, located in the Andes Mountains of Peru. That silver was the most abundant that had ever been located and insured an unlimited flow of all denominations of silver coins.

In fact, in 1575, Potosi was granted the right to have its own mint in order to convert silver bullion into a consistent form that could be shipped back to Spain.

Spain looked upon the new viceroyalties of Mexico and Peru as sources for great wealth. The eight-reales coins represented silver that had been refined, weighed, and made into a form that was both consistent in content and easily handled. Large quantities were placed in the holds of ships already laden with spices, sugar, quantities of wood, and similarly valuable cargo.

Spain lost many of these pieces of eight to pirates who hid in wait in unchartered waterways and little-known islands in the West Indies. Yet the ironical part of these losses was the fact that Spain indirectly created the need for pirates.

The Spanish Government wanted total control of all its citizens who were forming colonies in the New World. Although supplies were seldom adequate for the colonists, the Spanish Government would not allow the people to trade with other countries for what they needed. If an English vessel laden with cargo of value to the colonists were to try to sell to the people, the Spanish Colonial Government would be obligated to prevent the British from merchandising their wares. All supplies had to be of Spanish origin, regardless of whether or not serious shortages could have been eased by a relaxation of this regulation.

The colonists grew tired of such games and were angered by prices they felt were too high for the goods. They became ripe for black-market purchases, and this was when pirating developed as a well-paying profession.

The pirates would rob ships heading for Europe, then sell the goods at low cost to the colonists. When France and England enjoined their colonists from trading with any but the mother country, their colonists also took to the black market. Thus the restrictive trade policies resulted in the pirates' having a ready market for all the goods they could steal.

From 1580 through 1732, the Spanish mints in the New World relied upon one of the crudest approaches to the coinmaker's art of any country in the world. The silver bars, cast from refined bullion, were sliced into appropriately sized pieces. The pieces were hand-formed to a reasonably circular design that was consistent in weight, size, thickness, etc., from piece to piece. Then the appropriate markings were struck on the coins with hammers. It was a primitive system, which resulted in these early pieces, known as "cob" coinage (in reference to the manufacturing process), being crudely struck. Many of the markings are off-center, often to such a degree that parts of the designs are missing. The surfaces are often rough and uneven. Only a few of the earliest coins were even dated.

In 1572, Spain authorized the mints to greatly increase their production of eight-reales coins. The Spanish Government was deeply in debt. Inflation was out of control and wars had depleted the treasury. They needed the silver-bullion coins for paying their debts.

The fate of the eight-reales coins was twofold. Many were melted after being sent to Europe. England, France, and other nations recognized them for what they were—a convenient method for transporting silver of a known quality. The various businessmen receiving these pieces routinely melted them for their silver value.

The remainder of the coins found their way North into what would become the United States and Canada. The need for coins in these rapidly colonizing areas and the proximity to the Mexican and Peruvian mints made the pieces of eight a natural for British colonial commerce. In fact, so popular were these coins that they remained in legal use in the United States until the middle of the nineteenth century. They became the standard for trade with the Orient as well, and many American traders accumulated as many as possible specifically for use in the Far East. The only coin that ever challenged the supremacy of the eight-reales piece was the American trade dollar discussed in the previous chapter. However, the U.S. trade dollar was only struck for a few short years, and the eight-reales coins circulated for centuries.

The full coin history of Mexico is too involved for the scope of this book. For those interested in studying the field in depth, a list of further reading materials is found at the end of this volume. However, I will touch on important changes that occurred in Mexican coinage over the years, since this is an area that is quite popular with American collectors.

Around 1732, Mexican coinage underwent a dramatic change. The mint equipment became more modernized. In place of hand-stamping the coins, the mint installed a screw press that could exactly align the design on the blank silver planchet. These presses were powered by mills and the new coins were commonly called "milled" pieces.

As befit a new minting process, the eight-reales coins struck from the screw press were redesigned. The reverse shows the Pillars of Hercules on either side of two overlapping hemispheres of the world. A crown is on top of the globes and the ocean is below them. The latter was meant to symbolize the watery link between the New World and Europe.

By the 1750s, Mexico was troubled by a lack of small change. Copper coins were supposed to handle this problem but had never been produced to any degree because of the early hostility toward the coins. As a result, a number of businesses began making private copper tokens they could value at various fractions of a real—generally one eighth to one sixteenth. These went by the names pilones, tlacos, and sehales. These were outlawed in 1814 when the viceroy of the area ordered copper coins, called cuartos, to be issued as replacements.

Other parts of South and Central America were issuing coins during this same general time period. There were mints in Caracas, San Domingo, Santiago de Chile, and Guatemala. The coins were generally patterned after the cobs coming from Mexico and Peru in that they were originally cut from a bar of silver.

The history of Mexico has been a history of oppression and violent death. The Aztecs believed in human sacrifice to the gods, a bloody practice that probably made the victims wish they were atheists. Then the Spanish enslaved the people and forced them to labor for a ruler they had never seen and had no reason to respect. Even in more modern times, land has often been placed in the hands of the few, and one large group of citizens or another has faced extensive oppression.

No people ever become tolerant of tyranny, no matter how much a part of their history it may be. As a result, the Mexicans have periodically revolted, fighting back against their oppressors, regardless of the odds. The first time this occurred on a large scale was in 1810, during the Spanish rule. At that time, a priest named Miguel Hidalgo y Costilla, whose parish was in Dolores, Mexico, decided to gather the people together in revolt. He wanted the land returned to the Indians from whom it had been stolen and he wanted a congress to govern Mexico instead of the all-powerful viceroy. He remained loyal to the Spanish Government despite this rebellious attitude and felt that the congress should continue to serve under Ferdinand VII. This plan might have eventually proven acceptable to the mother country except for the fact that Ferdinand VII had been forced from the throne in favor of Joseph Bonaparte, a puppet leader under the thumb of his brother Napoleon.

On September 16, 1810, Father Hidalgo and a large number of his parishioners formed an "army" equipped with farming tools, rocks, and sticks. They traveled for eight days, finally reaching Guanajuato, where they fought and destroyed a group of Spanish soldiers. Although Hidalgo was a man of peace, his men looted the town and used excessive violence against anyone who tried to stop them. They also made the mistake of not continuing their march against the troops who dominated New Spain when they still had the element of surprise on their side. Instead, they celebrated their small victory and went home happily. Hidalgo eventually was captured, expelled from the Church, and killed.

Before Hidalgo's death, the treasury of Guanajuato was looted and a large quantity of silver bullion was taken. Hidalgo arranged to obtain the equipment and skilled personnel needed to turn the silver into coins. To insure that the money could be spent by the group, they imitated the Mexican money legitimately in circulation. The imitation was so close that the coins were indistinguishable.

On October 15, 1810, Hidalgo again had coins made, this time in a crude form and stamped with the designation "8 R," to indicate the value of eight reales, and "P.V.," to indicate they were provisional issues. These were made in Valladolid from silver objects stolen from the Church. The coins have apparently not survived, however.

A commemorative coin honoring Padre Miquel Hidalgo y Costilla.

The revolution, which seemed to lose momentum when Hidalgo went home, was refueled by the spirit of another Catholic priest, José Maria Morelos y Pavon. He raised an army under orders from Hidalgo and took it to the South of Mexico on October 20, 1810. Unfortunately, he won a few battles, then changed tactics rather than moving for complete victory over the Spanish. He formed what amounted to an Indian republic, where the land would be returned to the people. He also renounced the special privileges he and other members of the clergy had received over the years. But before his plans could be placed into action, soldiers caught up with him, killing him two months later.

Morelos did manage to leave a series of coins of the revolution to collectors. He created coins wherever he could find metal and the equipment for striking them. Pieces are known in silver, copper, and even some in gold.

From the time of Morelos' death through 1813, there were other rebellions, with some of the rebels creating provisional coins of different types. A few were struck in Oaxaca, and these are among the most common surviving. Many are priced well below fifty dollars and are quite popular with collectors. Other issues are great rarities, costing several hundred dollars on those few occasions when they can be located for sale.

The revolutionary battles did little to change the government but they did change the method of coining money. The seizure of bullion by the rebels caused severe coin shortages. After 1813, the Spanish rulers decided to open a number of branch mints in different parts of Mexico. These alleviated the problem of trying to ship coins throughout the land and speeded the distribution of coins to the businesses that needed them.

It is interesting to note that when Mexico finally did win freedom from Spain, the man who led the troops, Augustin de Iturbide, had been a Spanish loyalist who helped put down

Eight-reales coins struck under General Morelos in 1813.

A number of coins were produced during the period of the Mexican "Empire," several of which show Iturbide looking much like a Roman Emperor on the coins of that ancient nation. Copper, silver, and gold coins were all struck, the gold being the greatest rarities.

The Mexican Congress decided that if Iturbide was typical of the leadership possible with an empire, it was time to form a republic. A constitution was drafted, but this only led to dissension among different political factions. By 1857, the country was again enduring civil violence and what was known as the War of the Reform. So much money was spent to finance the military effort to unite the country that it could not meet its debts. Mexico was in turmoil, and the French Government took advantage of the situation. The French helped establish the second Mexican "Empire" under an Austrian named Maximilian.

Ferdinand Maximilian was officially an archduke in Austria but was actually a ne'er-do-well who was convinced his one chance for glory was as the leader of Mexico. His wife, Carlota, was an ambitious woman who delighted in being an Empress.

The only people who wanted Ferdinand to lead Mexico were the French. The United States wouldn't recognize his position and the people of Mexico were united in their hostility, even though fighting among themselves over what type of government they wanted in his place. Finally, in 1865, four years after Maximilian took the reigns of government, the United States ordered the French to leave Mexico under the terms of the Monroe Doctrine. The U. S. Government would have acted sooner had the country not been torn by its own Civil War.

By 1867, the French influence in Mexico was at an end. Maximilian was killed and Carlota returned to Belgium. The strain of all the violence she had witnessed and the realization that her moment of glory was over proved too much for her. She went insane and ended her days under the care of her family.

the insurrections of 1810–13. He established an independent Mexican Empire and was declared to be "Iturbide Augustin I" of Mexico in 1822. Unfortunately for him, his popularity waned immediately and he abdicated the following year, going into European exile. He returned to Mexico in 1824, but his successor had him killed.

It is interesting to note that Carlota left her mark on Mexican coinage. During her husband's reign, he expressed the belief that his portrait should not be used on the coinage. However, at her insistence, coins of fifty centavos, one peso, and twenty pesos were issued with Maximilian's portrait. These are dated 1866 and 1867 (the one-peso coin is the only one with the 1867 date).

The 1866 one-peso coin with Maximilian's likeness.

Mexico went on the decimal system of coinage in 1863, when the first coins of one centavo and five and ten centavos were issued. In the next several years, a full-decimal coinage was introduced at the various mints. To make this system easier for the people, it was related to the old Spanish system. Thus the new peso coin was equivalent to the Spanish eight reales, like the American dollar. A four-reales coin was equal to the new fifty-centavos denomination, and the two-reales coins were equal to the twenty-five-centavos coins. You may recall that the pieces of eight were often cut into bits, two bits or two reales, to be more exact, equaling twenty-five centavos or twenty-five cents in the United States. Thus the expression, "Shave and a haircut—two bits."

The public had trouble adapting to the new system at first. Not only were the decimal coins in short supply, but also the real coins had the same design as the early five- and ten-centavos pieces of 1867–69, even though the coins were not an exact match in terms of value. It was not until 1869 that major design changes were made and the confusion ended.

There were other changes going on in the rest of South and Central America during the first half of the nineteenth century. General Simón Bolivar and General San Martin led armies who battled the Spanish loyalists in Peru. Other military leaders also dealt severe blows to the Europeans and, by 1826, the lands were free from Spanish domination. The countries of Bolivia, Chile, Colombia, La Plata, Paraguay, and Peru were established as independent nations. Each country established its own coinage, primarily featuring the portraits of the rebels who led them to independence.

The last great period of violence occurred at the turn of this century. Sebastian Lerdo was President of Mexico in 1872, succeeding the late Benito Juarez, a popular leader who had helped oust the French from Mexico. Lerdo had only limited support from the army, however, and in May 1877 General

Porfirio Diaz triumphantly took control of the country.

Diaz was determined to make Mexico a world power. He improved international relations, increased trade, and helped modernize the country. Unfortunately, his internal record was as exploitive as that of many of his predecessors. A handful of influential men were given ninety-six million acres of land that should have gone to the Indians. He had disdain for the rights of the poorer people and angered many of his countrymen.

A number of men spoke out against President Diaz, including the unlikely Francisco Madero, a member of the wealthy, privileged minority. Madero felt the people were being exploited and should share the nation's wealth. He was jailed for his opposition, then forced into exile, though not before there were many who adopted his views.

One of the unusual rebels against the government's oppression was the famous Mexican bandit Pancho Villa. He began leading armed bands of guerrillas, as did a peasant named Emiliano Zapata.

Eventually rioting and organized violence were occurring throughout the country. In each city, the army was either overwhelmed or sympathetic, but whichever the case in a particular area, the mobs always triumphed. Diaz fled and Madero returned as the new President.

Madero's triumph was short-lived. He had written a book before his arrest by the men over whom he emerged victorious, and the writing gave the impression he would move quickly to reinstate human rights. He procrastinated on the redistribution of the wealth, however, and the people cared little about his philosophy. If he was going to be slow putting his words into action, they did not want to bother with him. Another revolt occurred, this time led by a soldier named Victoriano Huerta, who had Madero murdered.

Huerta lacked the following he had hoped for, and numerous men, including Pancho Villa and others among the revolutionaries, began fighting his government. There was no cohesiveness, however, and the rebel leaders also fought each other. In seven years, from 1913 through 1920, Mexico had ten different Presidents as a result of this divisiveness.

Collectors are not so much interested in the internal struggles for power that shattered Mexico during this period as they are with the coins that emerged. Rebel groups frequently seized precious metal and produced their own coins. For example, in 1913, one rebel group was operating in the state of Chihuahua in the area known as Parral. The Parral–Santa Barbara Railway was headquartered there and a storage area had a large quantity of copper wire. The copper was seized and used to produce two-centavos coins. Larger-denomination silver coins were also made, many of which have gold mixed in with the silver.

Pancho Villa produced what may be the most famous of all Mexican Revolution coins. This is a coin that reads "MUERA HUERTA" or "Death to Huerta." It was dated 1914 and was considered the ultimate insult against the government leader. Huerta was so incensed that he considered anyone who would accept such a coin in change to be his mortal enemy. He ordered his followers to murder anyone seen holding or trying to pass one of these "death" coins.

By 1920, Mexico was again at peace. The United States of Mexico had been established and the coinage became stable. The metal content changed drastically, however.

When Mexico was the prime source of silver for the world, the value of the metal was consistent and coin quality could be maintained. The ratio of silver to gold on the world market was reasonably stable.

Then came a change in the fortunes of the world. Silver was discovered elsewhere, especially in Nevada, where the Comstock Lode made the Mexican sources seem almost minor. Silver coins became abundant and the premium paid for silver drastically declined.

The death coin.

sixteen ounces of silver equaling one ounce of gold no longer prevailed. The Mexican coins grew less and less valuable.

Mexico gradually reduced the quantity of silver in its coins and the physical size of the peso. At first this was a matter of convenience and a way of insuring that circulating coins would be of value as money only and not as bullion pieces. Then, in 1935, when the United States went off the gold system, silver rose in value. The Mexicans continued to reduce the amount of this metal used in their coins, recognizing that if they maintained the silver, the rising prices would make it more profitable to melt the coins than to spend them. By 1970, Mexican pesos were made from a combination of copper and nickel. Silver was not used at all.

Many of the Mexican coins of recent times are visually unexciting. Most have portraits of the various leaders who were involved in the numerous struggles for independence. Father

This coin of Mexico shows Dona Josefa Ortiz de Dominguez, an early Mexican patriot determined to help her people become independent. She is one of the few women thus honored by a country.

Then several European nations went on the gold standard, downgrading silver in their monetary system. Even worse, in those parts of the world where silver dollar-sized coins remained desirable, most notably the Far East, the Mexican peso was no longer dominant. As a result, the silver-to-gold ratio of

Hidalgo has been honored, for example, as were Madero, Diaz, and others.

There have also been some commemoratives, many of which are quite attractive. A steam railroad engine is featured on one five-peso silver coin of 1950. The Pyramid of the Sun is seen on the twenty-cent piece introduced in 1943. A winged figure of Liberty is found on the two-peso coin of 1921 commemorating Mexican independence. And in 1968, the Nineteenth Olympic Games were honored.

Gold coins have also been issued by Mexico, the fifty-peso coin being a popular one with bullion buyers who purchase gold for its intrinsic worth rather than as a collector's item. The 1947 Mexican fifty-peso coin has been restruck in modern times with no difference in the date or design. The restrikes were meant strictly for purchase by bullion buyers, not collectors. The 1947-dated coins compete with one-ounce gold coins struck by South Africa, Austria, and other countries offering similar bullion species.

The change in the value of the peso has made many Americans living along the Mexican border get into the Mexican collecting habit. Many coins sold by Mexican dealers and available through Mexican banks just inside the country are extremely inexpensive compared with just a few years ago. Thus a large quantity of attractive coins can be accumulated even by those with a limited budget.

Chapter 4

COINS FROM AROUND THE WORLD

At the opening of this book, the subject of the world's earliest coins was discussed. Since this chapter will explore the coins issued by the various nations of the world, it is a good point for reviewing ancient coins as collectors' pieces. These coins exist in large numbers, are available from many dealers, and frequently are quite inexpensive. Although ancient gold and silver coins from Greece and Rome can cost many thousands of dollars, a large number of the coins, particularly those made from bronze, can be purchased for from five dollars to ten dollars. If your area dealers do not stock them, they can be obtained by mail through a reading of the advertisements listed in the publications mentioned at the back of this book. Thus you can enjoy owning these fascinating coins even if you have a modest budget and your area dealers do not stock them.

The Lydians are credited with producing the first objects known as coins, but it was the ancient Greeks who developed the art of design on these tiny pieces of metal. They used none of the special reduction techniques now handled by machines. Instead, they worked with crude tools, producing images with details so fine we need a magnifying glass to fully appreciate the work.

The early Greek coins depicted the gods and goddesses in many forms. Animal symbolism was common, for example. The gods were believed to be able to appear as different animals. Zeus could turn himself into an eagle, and Athena could become an owl. The city of Athens, whose patron goddess was Athena, issued coins with owls as the main design for this reason.

As the coinage art advanced, more elaborate designs were executed. The city of Syracuse introduced coins that honor Agon, god of the Games, by showing him in his chariot pulled by a team of four horses. To complete this elaborate design, Nike, the winged symbol of victory, is shown flying overhead with the winner's crown he is going to place on the head of the triumphant chariot racer.

The Greeks relied primarily on silver for their coins. Gold was used upon occasion but only as a last resort when silver was scarce. Gold coins were not desired, and their issuance reflected internal problems within the

The earliest coins of the ancients had symbolic figures rather than likenesses of real people.

A tetradrachm showing the winged horse.

An ancient owl tetradrachm of Athens struck between 490 and 430 B.C.

A tetradrachm with the head of Athena.

cities that had to produce them to satisfy coinage needs.

The coin designers took great pride in their work and made certain that their names or initials appeared somewhere on the coins. Often they were hidden in the hair of a goddess. At other times they appeared on a tablet carried by one of the figures rendered on the coin. Coins were a new art form for the people, and the men who produced the best designs earned

A Thessalian Confederacy coin showing a double-victoriate head of Zeus, struck sometime between 196 and 146 B.C. in ancient Greece.

great respect. It was natural for them to want to "sign" their metal "canvases."

Vanity was as great among the ancient Greeks as it is today. One of the more popular ways in which it revealed itself was in the styling of hair. Women tended to wear their hair long, working it into elaborate shapes. The coins depict these styles on the various goddesses and, later, on the women of power who were honored by the Emperors.

The early Greek coinage was not co-ordinated except in terms of the values placed on the coins. Each city created its own designs. Sometimes these were highly original. At other times they were imitations of designs seen on coins brought by traders from other areas. But there was no consistency of design from mint to mint.

The first break with the independent-city mint tradition came under the rule of Philip II, father of the conquerer who would become known as Alexander the Great. Philip

believed that coinage should be representative of the nation, not of different mint designers. He ordered several Greek mints to strike identical designs to achieve this end.

Philip II was assassinated in 336 B.C. after conquering all of Greece. He was making preparations for the conquest of Asia Minor when he died and it was natural for his son, Alexander, to want to go forth and accomplish what his father had begun. Alexander had himself proclaimed the leader of all the Greek states in 334 B.C., then led his armies in a war against the Persian Empire.

Alexander the Great's military conquests are well known, but his contribution to coins is not so familiar. He was the first leader to have his portrait on a coin. Prior to his rule, only the gods could be so honored. However, an idealized portrait of Alexander began appearing on the coinage of Lysimachus, a former general who served under Alexander.

There were several reasons why the rulers liked the new freedom to place their portraits on coins. One was that it linked them with the gods in the eyes of the public. Coin portraits gave the impression the rulers were in the league with the immortals, and this further enhanced their power.

Another reason the rulers liked having their heads on coins was the vanity of it. They enjoyed letting their image be seen by all the people of the land. This also served as an educational tool because the coin portraits were often the only way the public could know the appearance of their rulers.

Portraits that appeared on coins often told stories that are somewhat unusual. One coin of Parthia showed the head of the beautiful Musa, one of the most ruthless women of her day. She was a slave girl whom Caesar Augustus presented to King Phraates IV. The King was so taken with her looks that he married her and placed her on the throne, an action she cherished. However, as time passed, Musa seemed to feel that her influence in government was diminishing. Her looks were fad-

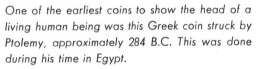

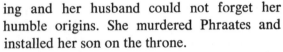

One of the earliest coins to show the head of a living human being was this Greek coin struck by Ptolemy, approximately 284 B.C. This was done during his time in Egypt.

ing and her husband could not forget her humble origins. She murdered Phraates and installed her son on the throne.

The Roman coinage evolved from that of the Greeks, and some of the early concepts are similar. Thus gods, animals, and renderings of games such as the chariot races abound on early Roman specie.

The earliest Roman coins were crude hunks of metal. Gradually these were replaced by ingots made from bronze and weighing three to five pounds each (*aes signatum*—marked bronze—was their name). Finally a currency system based on a one-pound bronze piece was established. This pound was known as an *aes grave*—heavy bronze. The basic coin was called an *aes* and was made equal to twelve *unciae*. One *unciae* translates roughly to one ounce, the more familiar, modern term. The other values included a *semis* or half-pound coin, and the *tremis,* which was two ounces. This system was utilized in approximately the fourth and third centuries B.C., well before the time of the Roman Empire.

The gods were extremely important to the Romans. They sought their protection, divine grace, guidance, and favor. Thus it was natural for them to issue coins showing Jupiter holding a scepter and driving his chariot. Juno was also shown, and it is from her full name— Juno Moneta—that our word "money" evolved. She was the protector of the Roman Mint.

The coins showed other gods as well. Apollo, Diana, Luna, Hercules, and many more made their appearance on the ancient gold, silver, and bronze pieces.

Legends found their way onto the coins of Rome. The rape of the Sabine women appears on one "X rated" coin. Others show the founding of Rome, Romulus, and numerous other scenes.

The Romans recognized the value coins could play in educating the public to the

A coin of Augustus shown actual size. The reverse shows the god Apollo holding his lyre.

events of the day. When a new building was erected, a new leader in power, a war fought, or games played, coins would be struck showing these events. The coinage became similar to a newspaper, conveying information throughout the land. When the Roman Empire was established, the people in the far reaches were able to learn all about leaders they might never see in person just by studying the coins.

One example of a "newspaper" coin is a piece struck by Hadrian. It shows the Emperor marching while wearing military dress and carrying a baton. He is followed by three soldiers and the "pretorian prefect" or military commander. The men are obviously engaged in military activity, a design meant to reassure the people. Hadrian was known as a man who tried to avoid war. However, he used the coins to show the people that he was regularly having the army practice maneuvers so they could adequately defend the people if an enemy attacked.

The Romans had a huge arena known as a circus where horse, chariot, and foot races were held, along with a number of other sports. Spectators lined three sides of the large structure, with the Emperor's seat carefully positioned so he could see everything that went on in the arena.

The Circus Maximus of Rome was the largest of the circus structures and was periodically made even bigger. It held anywhere from 150,000 to 385,000 spectators, depending upon which Emperor was in power and took the time to add to the structure.

How do we know so much about the various circuses? Although there are written records, a primary source is the design on ancient coins.

Three Roman coins depicting the Circus Maximus.

Numerous coins show different views of the circus and the events taking place therein. These coin designs enabled the average Roman to have knowledge of what was happening in the greatest athletic arena of the day.

The Roman coins also gave the public an indication of who was in power. Since the Emperor was hostile to those who did not support him, and since many of the people were far away from Rome, they relied on coin portraits to tell them who had control at any given time. This enabled the people to declare their support for the right person when he happened to be in their city. Otherwise they might have continued expressing loyalty to someone who had been assassinated, unknown to them, putting their own lives in jeopardy.

Because the Romans placed the portrait of the person in power on the obverse of their coins and lesser figures on the reverse, we have an ancient example of a woman's fight for power through coinage. When Nero rose to the position of Emperor, his ambitious mother, Agrippina, tried to manipulate him any way she could, including by having incestuous relations with him. He made her his coruler during his first year, placing her portrait near his own on the *obverse* of his coins.

Nero's interest in his mother waned. The second year in power resulted in Agrippina's portrait being banished to the *reverse*. Then, as she totally lost favor with her son and he plotted to murder her, he removed her image entirely. Smart politicians, far from the gossip of Rome, knew how to act toward the Emperor's mother by a careful study of each new issue of coins.

Even military tactics have been broadcast by way of coins. The Roman Republic triumphed over a group of Arverni warriors led by a man named Bituitus. The Arverni warriors used large dogs in the battle, something unknown to the Romans. The battle was shown on coins, the dogs drawn almost as large as a man so the people could see what they had to endure in the conflict.

The Romans took pride in making portraits that were as accurate as possible. Every facial defect is likely to be shown on their coins, a fact that has led a Canadian doctor/coin collector to diagnose numerous illnesses such as goiter as being prevalent among the people. The one disappointing part of accurate coin portraiture is that it shatters present-day illusions. For example, the coins of Cleopatra, the "siren" of Egypt who shared her bed with Caesar and Mark Antony, reveal her to be a

This coin of Nero, shown actual size, bears the triumphal arch. It was erected in A.D. 62 when Rome conquered Parthia. Only much later did Nero learn that the victory was a false one. His soldiers had lost. Since the arch was in the process of being erected, Nero said nothing and let it be completed.

This coin of Nero (shown actual size) has a reverse featuring Ceres. Opposite her is Annona, the goddess of plenty. Ceres holds corn ears in her right hand and a torch in her left. These coins were issued during the period of hunger in the land and represented Nero's great willingness to share his food with the people.

rather homely woman. She certainly was not the beauty Elizabeth Taylor portrayed when her story was made into a movie many centuries later.

Many of the Emperors tried to increase their wealth by debasing the coins. They would use less and less precious metal, some going to the extreme of producing bronze coins with a silver wash meant to fool the public into thinking the coins were solid silver. Frequently the government used debased coins when paying its debts and demanded pure silver and gold coins when the public paid taxes.

The situation became so serious that the public lost all faith in coins. Prices soared and many people took to using barter as a means of handling their debts. The economy was in chaos by the end of the third century A.D., and some sort of control was definitely needed.

The answer to the problem came with Emperor Diocletian. In A.D. 301, Diocletian announced wage and price controls as well as a return to coinage of real value. Before listing the changes to be made, Diocletian issued a statement that might have been spoken by someone today. He said, in part:

"Who is so dim-witted or so devoid of human feeling that he cannot have known or noticed that all salable objects offered for sale or traded in towns have increased so much in price that unbridled greed is no longer restrained even by a superfluity in the market or a good harvest? The men who are behind this business are vexed beyond endurance when the fortunate earth is moistened by rain from heaven as earnest of future fruitfulness, since they only pity themselves when favorable weather promises a rich harvest. These men, who have nothing better to do than carve up the benefits sent by the gods for their own advantage, damming up the open-handed favor of heaven and in bad years trading in seed corn and cornering the market, these men, who think only of their gain and their per cent: subjects!—it is to forbid these men the

practice of their greed that we are called by our care for humanity."

The actual price scales cannot be translated into current dollars and cents. However, an effort has been made that at least details the relative value fixed for services. Some of the earnings for different skills per day are:

Unskilled workman	$ .108
Bricklayer	$ .216
Carpenter	$ .216
Stonemason	$ .216
Blacksmith	$ .216
Shipbuilder	$ .216
Painter	$ .324
Barber (per shave)	$ .009
Gymnastic teacher (per pupil, per month)	$ .216
Employee to watch children (per month)	$ .216
Lawyer presenting case	$1.09
Lawyer for finishing case	$4.33

There were also a number of specialized skills that had varying rates. For example:

Teachers, per pupil, per month	$.22 plus food
Teachers in arithmetic	$.33 plus food
Teachers in Greek or geometry	$.87 plus food

Such men as scribes, tailors, and coppersmiths were paid on a piecework basis.

When it came to food, eggs were $.051 cents a dozen. A quart of beer cost $.015, common wine ran $.06 a quart, and fine wine of Picenum, Tibur, and Falernum cost $.22 a quart.

Pork was one of the more expensive meats at $.073 cents a pound. A pound of beef cost $.049, as did mutton. Ham was the costliest, at $.12 a pound.

Five heads of lettuce, 5 cabbages, or 10 turnips all could be purchased for $.017. For $.026 you could buy 25 asparagus stalks.

Salt was one of the most expensive necessities, at $.745 a bushel.

Clothing could get quite expensive, depending upon your position in life. A pair of trousers cost $.087, but a first-quality storm coat cost $21.76. A first-quality pair of boots ran $.52, while a patrician's shoes ran $.65.

Other clothing was costly as well. A first-quality military mantle ran $17.40, while a first-quality undergarment ran $8.70.

Even the goods for making clothing could be high. Genuine purple silk cost the astronomical sum of $652.20 per pound. Genuine purple wool was somewhat less, at $217.40 per pound. White silk was the cheapest, at just $52.22 per pound.

Diocletian's action greatly reduced the problem of rampant inflation. However, the days of the Roman Empire were numbered by then. The Emperor prevented a total collapse of the economy but financial situation continued to gradually deteriorate over the following years.

There are any number of ways to collect ancient coins. Some people collect the coins at random, enjoying the thrill of knowing that the coin being studied under a magnifying glass might be one that Jesus once carried in his pocket or some great military leader spent for lodging.

Other collectors have a theme in mind. Some collect only those Greek coins that have animal symbols. Some collect coins of the twelve Caesars who ruled Rome. Still others specialize in coins depicting gods or warfare or images of some of the wonders of the ancient world that no longer exist. The approach can be totally your own, for there is no right or no wrong way to choose. If your collection of ancient coins gives you pleasure, then the way you are obtaining them is "right" for you.

Before progressing in our look at world coins, a word of warning is in order. If you eventually decide to invest in coins (and a chapter of this book covers that subject), you should take care to have all ancient coins purchased as investments carefully authenticated. Over the years numerous counterfeiters have been active. One, a man named Becker, produced coins that take a highly trained eye to discern. It is doubtful that the average collector could spot many of these counterfeits. Thus it is best that you seek expert advice before risking large sums of money. Ancient coins can be good investments but not if the coin you buy proves to be an imitation.

As the Roman Empire faded into history, the Byzantine Empire of the East was coming into its own. For coin collectors, however, the Byzantine Empire represents a step backward. The coins, though interesting, were extremely crude. The engravers made no effort to create a realistic coinage design. All work was symbolic, revealing little about the character of the people portrayed.

Byzantine coinage was based in large measure on the values of the Roman coins that were part of what was then the world's best-known money system. The Romans had a gold coin known as a solidus, for example. The Byzantines issued the same type of gold coin, though with a different design. It became known as a "nomisma." From its inception in the eighth century A.D. until the eleventh century A.D., the nomisma maintained a fairly constant gold standard. After that peroid, the gold content was diminished by mixing it with other metals as the rulers tried to make additional profits, much the same as the Roman gold had been debased.

There were Byzantine copper and silver coins, often richly ornamented despite the crudeness of the renderings of the Emperor. The one new design element was the showing of the elaborate costumes popular with the Byzantine leaders. On some coins, the Emperor is shown with his clothing and symbols of office standing next to a rendering of the Virgin Mary, which added a religious aspect to the pieces. This is similar to the earliest portraits of Alexander, which were also meant to show a religious connection, though Alexander was a polytheist and the Byzantine leaders were Christians. In fact, some of the coins of Justinian II, who began his rule in A.D. 685, show the figure of Christ on the coins. The designation "Rex Regnantium" or "King of Kings" also appears.

Emperor Alexius I Comnenus, who ruled Byzantium from 1081 to 1118, made some radical changes in the coinage. Not only did he reduce the intrinsic value of the coins in order to make more money with the same amount of gold and silver, he also made rather crude, unusually designed coins. The gold nomisma, for example, was not only debased, it was also made cup-shaped and bore a crude portrait that made the Emperor look like a character on a children's puppet show.

The crudeness of the coins, which worsened into the middle of the fifteenth century, reflected the general decadence of the Byzantine Empire. Its decline became so severe that one fifteenth-century writer said of the luxuries once enjoyed by the rulers: "The jewels in the crown were glass, the robes not real cloth-of-gold but tinsel, the dishes copper, while all that appeared to be rich brocade was now only painted leather."

The Byzantine Empire fell to the Turks on May 30, 1453. Gold had long since vanished from the coins and only crude silver and copper pieces remained.

There were other coins circulating during the centuries following the fall of Rome. The Vandals, the Ostrogoths, and others all developed coinage for the lands they conquered. Most were based on the Roman concepts, though more crudely engraved and lacking in great intrinsic worth. When gold was issued, the coins were smaller than in the past because the metal was becoming increasingly scarce. A wide variety of issues came from France, Italy, and other territories as the years passed.

In addition to the decline in the quality of coinage, there was a diminished demand for this medium of exchange. Eighth-century feudal Europe had returned to a modified barter system. Coins were used but usually only to supplement a trade. One transaction of A.D. 768 that has been recorded indicates that a plot of land was bought that was valued at twenty-eight solidi. Only fifteen solidi in coinage were paid, however. The remaining amount owed was collected in the form of a horse. The animal was a key feature of the transaction, and there is a chance the deal would not have been made had coins, only, been offered.

Usually coins were overlooked entirely. A barter system relating to goods and services was the most common means of exchange, especially between the large landowners and the peasants who resided there. The very wealthy felt that jewels and Church plate were more secure forms of money than coinage and preferred to maintain such items for times of need.

The peasants were the primary users of coins and then only when they had surplus crops. Frequently they made a bare subsistence living. When they got ahead of themselves and could afford to buy a luxury or two from the city, coins were a convenient means of exchange. Coins were also valuable for trading between cities, though even here some barter was still practiced when the merchants of different communities each had goods the others wanted.

Charlemagne, the Emperor who conquered most of Europe in the late 700s and early 800s A.D., establishing what became known as the Holy Roman Empire, had a major impact on coins. He believed that coins should have a firm intrinsic worth and increased the weight of the standard pieces in use. Because his troops kept annexing territory, the coins struck upon his orders began circulating widely, becoming the standard for exchange throughout most of Europe. It was through his efforts that coinage began taking on greater importance than barter, providing the basis for a monetary system that has been developing ever since.

Most of Charlemagne's coins were silver,

and the designs were similar to the imperial coinage of the fallen Roman Empire. This may have been the result of Charlemagne's conquest of Italy and subsequently becoming Emperor in Rome in A.D. 805. Whatever the case, the coin engravings are far more sophisticated than that used by the Byzantines.

In A.D. 987, when Hugh Capet became Europe's major leader, coinage standards deteriorated. The designs became simplified, the cross and the ruler's name dominating the coin surface.

As can be seen, the Middle Ages was a period of turmoil in coin design. There were good, bad, and downright ugly designings taking place, with the intrinsic worth dependent upon the ruler's honesty. This period of several hundred years following the fall of the Roman Empire is one with which few coin collectors involve themselves. The history of the times is violent and colorful but the coinage is confusing and ugly. Many dealers avoid stocking such items entirely.

The most popular of all world coins is the "crown." This is a general term applied to dollar-sized silver coins. Crowns have been struck by various countries as far back as the fifteenth century.

The first crowns ever struck can be traced to Hapsburg Tyrol, an area that was part of the main trade route between Germany and Italy. The land was ruled by Archduke Sigismund, who established a mint in the territory known as Hall, where large deposits of silver had been discovered. The year was 1476 and Sigismund employed a Venetian named Antonio de Caballis, also known as Anthonis von Ross, to serve as mintmaster.

Von Ross was aware that Sigismund had been producing gold coins at a mint in Meran prior to the major silver discovery. However, von Ross thought the government should change and begin producing large silver coins equal in value to the gold coins that had been standard. Since large quantities of the metal were readily available, Sigismund agreed and,

in 1484, the mint began producing a silver coin known as a halbguldiner. This was followed by the guldiner in 1486, a coin that weighed exactly one ounce. It was the world's first "crown" or dollar-sized silver coin.

The advantage of the crown, beyond the worth of the silver, is that its large size offers the potential for the finest artwork possible on coins. There is room for exquisite detail and creativity of design, a challenge many engravers have successfully met over the years.

The 1486 guldiner.

The first guldiners leave much to be desired as artistic creations, even though they are among the nicest coins of their time. Archduke Sigismund is portrayed in all his glory, wearing the costume of his office on one side. On the other, his role as defender of the people is shown by having him appear in armor, mounted on a horse.

The gulden was the standard gold coin of the realm when the silver guldiners were introduced. It was hoped that since gold was scarce and silver was plentiful, the people would willingly make the change and utilize the guldiners in place of the gold. Unfortunately for Sigismund, the people did not trust the new coins and continued relying upon the gold for trade. As a result, the new guldiners seldom were circulated. They were used primarily for giving to important government and social leaders as gifts of state.

Except for a chance discovery of silver, the name of our current dollar coin might have been a variation on the word guldiner. However, in 1516, in the Bohemian territory known as Joachimsthal ("The Valley of St. Joachim"), a massive silver deposit was uncovered. The land was owned by the counts of Schlick, who were anxious to put this new wealth to work for them.

Count Stephen of Schlick (also spelled Šlik) made the decision that the coins should be large, much like the silver guldiners. They had the image of St. Joachim on the obverse and were rather crudely struck. However, more than two million were produced in the next eight years, and they became widely circulated and well known throughout that section of Europe. The coins were named for the area from which they came. They were called joachimsthaler, which most people shortened to "thaler." A corrupted spelling led to our present word "dollar."

It happened that the thaler was introduced at a time when large deposits of silver had been found throughout both Europe and the New World. As a result, many rulers began issuing the large crowns. Some went even farther, making two-thaler coins of elaborate design, such as one showing the departure of St. Ursula, a British princess who was martyred in an area near Cologne. She appears in a boat surrounded by a half dozen others on the two-thaler coin issued by Cologne.

The general term "crown" used to describe large silver coins dates to the 1520s and the coinage of Henry VIII of England. He had a stable monetary system but was forced to change the intrinsic worth of England's coins to match changes going on in Europe. The ratio of gold to silver had changed internationally, and Henry's gold coins were being shipped abroad for melting. Speculators found that they contained more gold than their face value indicated.

Henry reduced the amount of gold in his coins so their face value and intrinsic worth were in line with the coins of other countries. In fact, the coin was meant to be almost exactly the same as the French coin known as an "ecu." This new coin was called a "crown" and was valued at five shillings.

The gold coin was never very popular with the British people, but the name "crown" was. Since the gold coin was equal to five shillings, when a large silver coin of equal value was introduced—a coin the size of the thalers—it was immediately called a crown.

The designs found on the crowns of the world have made them one of the most popular of all coin issues. Collectors interested in the artistic side of coin collection delight in their variety. There is a Haitian crown featuring the image of the country's international airport, a plane flying overhead. And Western Samoa issued a crown honoring the Commonwealth Games. It shows two boxers in combat, their bodies so detailed you can almost detect the odor of sweat and blood.

Switzerland has a series of shooting talers featuring men in gaily colored costumes holding rifles along with various symbolic designs. St. George slaying the dragon is a prime feature on many of the Great Britain crowns.

Among the most unusual crowns are those of Equatorial Guinea. One, issued in 1970 in honor of the Olympics, has an elaborate design that includes images of the various countries which hosted the Olympic Games from 1952 through 1972.

A number of modern crowns, including the Equatorial Guinea piece just mentioned, fall into the category known as noncirculating legal tender. For years countries have made money with their postage stamps by issuing countless designs of interest to collectors rather than just trying to meet the needs of the mail service. As coin collecting increased in popularity, a number of countries decided to do with coins what they had done with stamps, and the result was noncirculating legal tender (NCLT).

What has happened is that a country will decide to issue a coin or a series of coins that are not needed for business purposes such as making change. These are struck in varying quantities but usually in the range of five thousand to thirty thousand pieces or somewhat more. They might be struck in silver or even gold, and the issue prices will be fairly high compared with intrinsic worth. Most will be in proof condition, a special method of striking coins utilizing highly polished dies in order to obtain a more impressive-looking design. Uncirculated coins will also be available, though these will be struck in the conventional manner. Such uncirculated pieces are less impressive than proofs.

Next the coins are marketed, sometimes by a major dealer and sometimes by the mint that makes them. Some NCLT coins are made by major mints in the various European countries. At other times they may be made by private mints that also offer medals, specially designed ingots, and other collector items. Usually it is only the private mints that take on world marketing chores. NCLT coins made by government mints often rely on coin dealers and special private marketing experts.

The NCLT coins are heavily advertised in both hobby journals and general-circulation publications. Direct-mail sales appeals may also be made. The price is fairly high—approximately twenty-eight dollars for a proof Western Samoa crown of six thousand mintage at this writing, for example. However, in many cases the entire issue sells out and there is a waiting list for the items. Their artistic designs make them popular despite the price.

Coin collectors generally want to collect only those coins that serve as money—legal-tender issues. A coin that is specially sold is not going to be spent and is little more than a medal. Rather than lose collector interest, the governments issuing NCLT coins go to elaborate lengths to make the items legal tender for purchase of goods at face value. However, the sham is obvious when you discover that many bankers within the countries issuing the NCLT coins have refused to accept the NCLT coin in exchange for circulating currency until it is proven to be legal tender. This has happened numerous times with gold coins in the NCLT category. No one in the issuing government bothered to let the nation's bankers know what the NCLT coins looked like, since it was assumed the buyers would never take them to the bank to exchange for the country's circulating currency.

The "noncirculating" part of the NCLT name means precisely what it says. The buyers of the coins put them in their collections. They do not circulate them.

Should you buy NCLT coins for your collection? Certainly, if you enjoy their beauty and don't mind the fact that they were never spent by the people of the country that issued them. However, their issue prices are high, resale value is often low, and they are scorned by the "purists" among coin collectors.

In recent years there has been talk about the United States issuing NCLT crowns—silver or clad dollars of copper and nickel sandwiched together with commemorative designs meant for collectors. Half-dollar commemoratives were issued for many years by this country and, though they were also NCLT, all of them are in great demand by collectors.

Some of the older foreign coins you can collect were once used in the fight against disease. This occurred primarily back during the sixteenth and seventeenth centuries, when medical knowledge was crude at best.

As an example of early medical "knowledge," charms were frequently the best "cures" for ailments, according to the "experts." If you had malaria, the "cure" was to seal a spider in a nutshell and hang it around your neck. One medical writer of the day talked about bloodstone, detailing its special healing properties by saying it ". . . stancheth blood, driveth away poison, preserveth health; Yea, and some maintain that it provoketh rain and darkeneth the sun, suffering not him that beareth it to be abused." Another charm was topaz, which ". . . healeth a lunatic person of his passion of lunacy and the garnet assisteth sorrow and recreates the heart."

The people firmly believed in various charm cures and the special powers of certain individuals, primarily those of royal blood. Doctors, however, were considered somewhat of a joke. One early writer talked about the medical profession, saying of doctors:

"When people acquaint him with their griefs and their ills, though he knows not what ails them no more than a horse, he tells them it is a scorbutick humor caused by a defluxion from the osscarum, afflicting the diapharagma and circoary-thenordal muscles! with which the poor old souls are abundantly satisfied, and wonder that he should hit on their distemper so exactly. He undertakes to spy out diseases, whilst they are yet lurking in their remotest causes! and has an excellent talent for persuading well people that they are sick, and by giving them his trash soon verifies the prediction. He especially succeeds in preying upon women, for he says, 'I never yet knew a female mind but ailed something when she came in presence of a doctor.'"

With such attitudes, it is easy to see why members of the royal family could be conceived to have the power to cure a dread disease known as the "King's evil." The disease, also called "scrofula," is now known to be a form of tuberculosis of the neck glands.

Edward the Confessor of England (A.D. 1004–66) was the earliest English King to touch people who were afflicted with illness in order to cure them. At least this is what has been recorded. However, since the story of his "cures" did not come out until his biography was written several years after his death, it is possible it was a fiction meant to give the royal family greater prestige in the eyes of the people. Whatever the case, the story was believed, and future rulers imitated the ceremony.

Queen Elizabeth I seemed to take great delight in coming into contact with her subjects. It was written that she touched "boldly and without disgust . . . handling them to health . . . herself worn with fatigue."

Coins became a part of royal touching during the reign of Charles II, who was an extremely active man of "medicine." Between May of 1662 and April of 1682, Charles II touched at least 92,107 individuals. This is somewhat unusual, since he was very interested in science and presumably would have tried to keep tabs on the people he "cured" to see how long they lived. Since this was a period in which the yearly death toll continued rising steadily despite his efforts, it is logical to think he would have questioned his powers, though apparently he didn't.

Charles II had coins struck to give each person he cured through his touching. They feature a ship in full sail and are similar to a charm coin his predecessor Edward III once had struck to protect the owner from harm on land and sea.

The coins Charles distributed to everyone he touched were made of gold. Since times were hard and many elderly people were going hungry, being cursed by the "King's Evil" became a profession in itself. Both sick and well went regularly for the "cure" in order to obtain the coins. Often the crowds were so large and boisterous that people were trampled to death. However, being in the midst of these throngs seemed worth the risk because by "taking the cure" repeatedly, the coins provided an ancient form of "Social Security" payment.

The King's intention was that the gold coins be worn by the person touched in order to increase the magic of the "cure." However, all the merchants looked upon them as money, though the design was different from general-circulation coins, and they were spent almost as soon as they were obtained.

Succeeding monarchs continued the royal touching and regularly passed out the coins. Some, like England's King William, thought the idea nonsense and only touched to please his subjects. However, even then he showed his cynicism by saying the words "God grant you better health and more sense."

Queen Anne, on the other hand, had no intention of physically contacting her subjects when she "touched." She utilized a lodestone, which she brushed against a "victim's" skin or body sores rather than touching the person with her fingers. She did not believe she had any special curative powers but assumed the ceremony was effective since the lodestone was believed to be able to draw out illness.

Royal touching was even Church-supported. The 1707 revision of the Book of Common Prayer featured a service of healing, which said that the mystery of the power was in "those secret rays of divinity that do attend Kings and Queens."

Most of the gold and, occasionally, silver touch coins remain in excellent condition despite the fact that some were holed for charms and considerably more were spent with merchants. The largest collection is in the British Museum, but many dealers have them in stock from time to time.

Another series of unusual British coins pop-ular with collectors are the Maundy coins. Maundy Thursday, the day before Good Friday, has long been a time for special celebration by the British. Beginning with the reign of Charles II (1660–85), four small silver coins —penny, twopence, threepence, and fourpence (groat)—were distributed to an equal number of men and women, the total number of people equaling the age of the monarch. The recipients were selected from among the poor, and the earliest coins were not dated. However, dating began in 1688, and the ceremony has continued into the twentieth century. Today the coins are purchased immediately by coin dealers who give the recipients many times the face value of the four pieces, secure in the knowledge that collectors are eager to purchase them for a substantial premium.

The coinage of Australia, New South Wales, and the rest of the area commonly called Australasia is interesting because of the curious circumstances of its settlement by the British. The British Government was extremely hostile to criminals back in the late 1700s, and the laws were such that almost anyone might be found guilty of a crime. What became minor offenses under legal revisions a century later were, in the late 1790s, crimes so serious that a convicted prisoner was subject to permanent exile.

It was during this period that Australia, New Zealand, and the surrounding area were first considered places where the British could increase their territory and also rid themselves of criminals. On August 17, 1786, Lord Sydney, the British Secretary of State for Home Affairs, announced that the territory first explored by Captain Cook sixteen years earlier would be used to relocate colonists. He stated, in part:

"I am, therefore, commanded to signify to your Lordships His Majesty's pleasure that you do forthwith take such measures as may be necessary for providing a proper number of vessels for the conveyance of 750 convicts to

Botany Bay, together with such provisions, necessaries, and implements for agriculture as may be necessary for their use after their arrival."

The early settlements were a nightmare. The several ships used for transportation took eight months to reach their destination. During this time, some of the convict passengers were treated decently by the men in command while others, on different vessels, were subject to torture, being chained for countless days at a time and other abuses. When they did arrive, the land was not so easy to work as had been thought, and a shortage of such necessities as foods containing Vitamin C resulted in diseases such as scurvy becoming rampant. It was not until the early 1800s that the settlements were showing signs of stability and self-support.

There was little money available for the Australasia settlements. Most coins came from the pockets of the soldiers and the prisoners, far fewer than were needed for commerce. Perhaps the best account of what happened was provided by Coleman Hyman who, in 1893, published a study entitled: *Account of the Coins, Coinages and Currency of Australia*. He stated, in part:

"While it is discouraging to find that the majority of writers on early Australian affairs pass over the matter of coins and currency without any reference, every established fact tends to show that though a very small amount of English money was used during the first few years after the arrival of 'the first fleet,' the majority of the dealings were arranged by barter: rum, corn, and other marketable produce being in high favour for the purpose of settling claims. Dollars also being recognized. The first form of Barter between the Settlers and the native appears (according to Governor Phillip's journal) to have been established at Parramatta in 1791, the settlers giving small quantities of rice or bread in exchange for fish, of which the natives frequently caught more than they required for immediate use."

Later in the text Hyman stated: "It may well be said the rummiest currency known was that initiated here when rum came to be so extensively used as a circulating medium. At first tacitly recognized by the authorities, in a few years this currency became a curse almost ineradicable; Governor Hunter forbade the bartering of spirits for grain, but, like many other orders, these were unheeded."

Coinage was a serious problem for the colonists, who were not permitted to make their own money. As other nations began to trade with the new settlement, the people used Spanish, Dutch, Indian, and English money interchangeably. A large quantity of copper coins were sent from England in 1800 to try to ease the difficulty, but it was nowhere near enough.

In 1813, the Governor of Australia tried to solve the coin shortage in a manner that was similar to the one used in Canada. Spanish dollars were as abundant in this land of former British criminals as they were in other parts of the world. The governor took the coins, had a hole punched in the center, and created his own holey dollars and dumps.

The holey dollars had the words NEW SOUTH WALES and the date placed on one side and the words FIVE SHILLINGS placed on the other. The small dumps were stamped with the name of the country on one side, similar to the larger coin, and the words FIFTEEN PENCE on the other.

Australia was no different from Canada in facing the counterfeiting problem. So many fake coins went into circulation that the public lost faith in the pieces, and their value in the marketplace dropped. By 1829, they ceased to circulate.

A rather humorous situation existed with the Maori of New Zealand. Social customs among these native people forced them to spurn material wealth. Whatever one native owned would be given away to friends as a sign of caring about others. Those who tried to hold onto possessions were scorned.

When the British colonists first arrived in New Zealand, they utilized barter with the natives. However, the natives did not really want to give up their material wealth and were delighted to discover the British coinage system. The reason was explained in *An Account of New Zealand* written by W. Yates in 1835. He said, in part:

"Barter of every description is now gradually giving way to the introduction of British coin and dollars. One powerful reason why natives preferred money to blankets, clothing, arms, and hardware, was that they were bound in honour to distribute it among their friends or, on the first cause of offence, to become dispossessed, but gold and dollars lie in so small a compass, that they can be easily concealed or carried undiscovered about their persons."

When Australia and New Zealand grew large enough to get their own mint, the coins designed for them were unusually interesting. The New Zealand coins of the 1730s, for example, feature different symbols relating to the land. The threepence pieces show crossed clubs, a symbol of the primitive people who once populated the area. The sixpence shows the native huia bird, the shilling showed a Maori warrior, and the florin also featured a native bird, the kiwi. An early New Zealand crown, struck in 1935 during the Silver Jubilee of George V, showed the King on the obverse and a Maori warrior shaking hands with a British naval officer on the reverse. At the bottom is the word "WAITANGI," which was the name of the treaty between the British and the natives that gave Britain control of the land.

A recent change in world coinage design came with the organization of the Food and Agriculture Organization (FAO) of the United Nations. In October of 1968, eleven countries prepared coins to mark the anniversary of FAO, all designs based on the theme "Grow more food for mankind." Most of these coins feature animals or food of various types as major design elements. A five-shilling coin of Uganda, for example, showed a cow grazing in a field while a calf nurses. The words PRODUCE MORE FOOD are underneath the rendering of the animals.

More than fifty countries began making FAO coins within five years of the earliest issues. Special albums were prepared to hold them, and these were sold through the Washington, D.C., office of the organization.

The FAO coins, which continue to be released from time to time by various countries of the world, were so popular with collec-

Some foreign coins tell unusual stories. This is the Chinese dollar of death. It was issued by General Chow, the governor of Kwiechow, located in the south of China. He issued this coin in the 1920s to honor a massive road-building effort. He wanted to have a coin with his picture on it, but that was considered improper to the Chinese. A man did not honor himself with such an act without actually causing disgrace. However, when the coin was issued, the grass underneath the car seemed to actually be Chinese letters spelling out the general's name. When the general was killed in such a car during one of the first rides on the road, it was believed that he was being punished for his arrogance in trying to gain fame.

tors that other methods for promoting this theme were tried. In 1971, a series of thirty Ceres medals were issued to honor the important women of the world as a means of stressing the role women play in meeting food needs. The list of those honored ranged from Indira Gandhi to Coretta Scott King to Margaret Mead to Shirley Temple Black. These medals have not met with such strong collector interest as the coins, however.

Western Samoa has a per-capita income of only around $350 to $400. Nevertheless, it manages to produce some of the most beautiful coins, which are then sold to collectors around the world. It is actually a better way to make money than using the coins for actual trade.

Almost any theme can be found on the coins of Europe and Asia. The coins of the British Commonwealth are among the most varied. Here are two examples: Cupid and his bow depicting the marriage of Philip and Elizabeth, and a King George VI commemoration.

Another example of a member of British royalty being honored. This time it was a coin of Gambia.

Austria, unlike many other countries, often has unusual reverses on its coins. This particular issue bears numerous shields relating to the country's history.

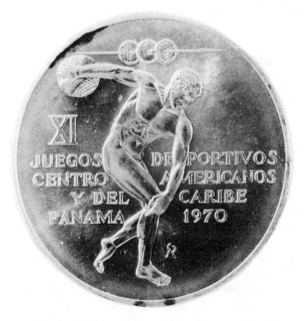

South and Central American coinage often has some of the highest-quality medallic art being produced. This beautiful Olympic figure was on a Panamanian coin of 1970.

Chapter 5

MOTTOES AND SYMBOLS

It would not seem that a coin motto could be controversial, but this proved the case with the words "In God We Trust" so familiar to American coin collectors. In fact, the attempt to remove this motto from our coins nearly cost Theodore Roosevelt his presidential support. But before we get to that story let us explore how the motto evolved.

Apparently the Reverend M. R. Watkinson, minister of the Gospel from Ridleyville, Pennsylvania, was the instigator of the religious-oriented motto for America's coinage. On November 13, 1861, with the Civil War just starting and the nation torn in two, he wrote to the Treasury Department with a suggestion. His letter stated, in part:

> One fact touching our currency has hitherto been seriously overlooked. I mean the recognition of the Almighty God in some form in our coins.
>
> You are probably a Christian. What if our Republic were now shattered beyond reconstruction? Would not the antiquaries of succeeding centuries rightly reason from our past that we were a heathen nation? What I propose is that instead of the goddess of liberty we shall have next inside the 13 stars a ring inscribed with the words "perpetual union"; within this ring the allseeing eye, crowned with a halo; beneath this eye the American flag, bearing in its field stars equal to the number of the States united; in the folds of the bars the words "God, liberty, law."
>
> This would make a beautiful coin, to which no possible citizen could object. This would relieve us from the ignominy of heathenism. This would place us openly under the Divine protection we have personally claimed. From my heart I have felt our national shame in disowning God as not the least of our present national disasters.
>
> To you first I address a subject that must be agitated.

The minister's letter seemed to fit with the thinking of the Treasury Secretary, who contacted the mint director on November 20, 1861, saying:

> No nation can be strong except in the strength of God, or safe except in His defense. The trust of our people in God should be declared on our national coins.
>
> You will cause a device to be prepared with-

out unnecessary delay with a motto expressing in the fewest and tersest words possible this national recognition.

The mint director complied. In December 1863, when designs for new one-, two-, and three-cent coins were prepared for the Treasury Secretary's approval, two different mottoes were also proposed. These were "God, our Trust" and "Our country; our God." Neither was satisfactory.

The Treasury Secretary finally sent a note to the mint director. It was dated December 9, 1863, and said:

> I approve your mottoes, only suggesting that on that with the Washington observe the motto should begin with the word "Our," so as to read: "Our God and our country." And on that with shield, it should be changed so as to read: "In God We Trust."

The Washington design to which there was reference meant a two-cent piece, which was being proposed. It would have had the first President's portrait, a concept that was changed to a wreath of wheat secured over a shield.

The motto "In God We Trust" became an accepted part of American coinage but was not required by law. Everyone felt that the motto was a good sign for the United States and thought little else about it.

In 1907, Augustus Saint-Gaudens was preparing his twenty-dollar-gold-piece design, which was considered the most beautiful ever created for an American coin. Both he and President Roosevelt, a lover of classical coinage, felt that the motto made no positive contribution and should be left off.

Roosevelt later explained his position in a letter to William Boldly. The letter was lost to history until its owner took it to the American Auction Association office of the California coin firm Bowers and Ruddy Galleries. There it was auctioned in December of 1975, the auction catalog having the text. The letter stated:

The motto "IN GOD WE TRUST" is now a standard fixture on all American coins. Here it is seen on the Standing-Liberty quarter.

An example of a typical coin of Saint-Gaudens.

When the question of the new coinage came up we lookt (sic) into the law and found there was no warrant therein for putting "IN GOD WE TRUST" on the coins. As the custom, altho without legal warrant had grown up, however, I might have felt at liberty to keep the inscription had I approved of its being on the coinage. But as I did not approve of it, I did not direct that it should again be put on. Of course the matter of the law is absolutely in the hands of Congress, and any direction of Congress in the matter will be immediately obeyed. At present, as I have said, there is no warrant in law for the inscription.

My own feeling in the matter is due to my very firm conviction that to put such a motto on coins, or to use it in any kindred manner, not only does no good but does positive harm, and is in effect irreverence which comes dangerously close to sacrilege. A beautiful and solemn sentence such as the one in question should be treated and uttered only with that fine reverence which necessarily implies a certain exaltation of spirit. Any use which tends to cheapen it, and, above all, any use which tends to secure its being treated in a spirit of levity, as is from every standpoint profoundly to be regretted. It is a motto which it is indeed well to have inscribed on our great national monuments, in our temples of justice, in our legislative halls, and in buildings such as those at West Point and Annapolis—in short, wherever it will tend to arouse and inspire a lofty emotion in those who look thereon. But it seems to me eminently unwise to cheapen such a motto by use on coins, just as it would be to cheapen it by use on postage stamps, or in advertisements. As regards its use on the coinage we have actual experience by which to go. In all my life I have never heard any human being speak reverently of this motto on the coins or show any sign of its having appealed to any high emotion in him. But I have literally hundreds of times heard it used as an occasion of, and incitement to, the sneering ridicule which it is above all things undesirable that so beautiful and exalted a phrase should excite. For example, thruout (sic) the long contest, extending over several decades, on the free coinage question, the existence of this motto on the coins was a constant source of jest and ridicule; and this was unavoidable. Everyone must remember the innumerable cartoons and articles based on phrases like "In God we trust for the other eight cents"; "In God we trust for the short weight"; 'In God we trust for the thirty-seven cents we do not pay"; and so forth, and so forth. Surely I am well within bounds when I saw that a use of the phrase which invites constant levity of this type is most undesirable. If Congress alters the law and directs me to replace on the coins the sentence in question the direction will be immediately put into effect; but I very earnestly trust that the religious sentiment of the country, the spirit of reverence in the country, will prevent any such notion being taken.

When the coins were released, the design was so new and different that the public studied it closely. Immediately the lack of the words "In God We Trust" was noticed and the reaction was swift. The editor of Pittsburgh's *United Presbyterian* wrote:

It would justify the striking of temperance laws and Sabbath laws from the statute-books of every State from the Atlantic to the Pacific. Because a good law is treated with disrespect by lawbreakers is no argument for its repeal. The principle advanced would justify the abrogation of the Ten Commandments. It is not so many years ago that one of the members of the United States Senate spoke to the Decalog as being an "iridescent dream." Would Mr. Roosevelt approve of the expunging of the Decalog because some men treat it with lightness and irreverence?

The Methodist religious journal, the *Christian Advocate,* also published in Pittsburgh, had a more tolerant editor. He stated:

On the whole, we believe he is right. At first thought some good people may not agree with him, but we believe that the more they consider the matter the more they will come to his way of thinking. At first we were unfavorably imprest (sic) by his action, but we have changed, and must now approve it. There is such a thing as making sacred things too common. Our religious faith should not be hidden in a napkin, but neither should it be too publicly and constantly paraded. It may thus be cheapened. Texts of Scripture may be degraded by unwise display, and being thrust into unseemingly places and connections. There are suitable times and places for such things, and there are some unsuitable. Opinions may differ as to whether the coin of the country is a proper place for the beautiful motto in question, but we believe the majority of the people will approve the President's act, and that Congress will not restore the motto.

The New York publication *American Hebrew* seemed to reinforce the attitude of the *Christian Advocate*. In an editorial, the periodical stated, ". . . the real quest on which should agitate the American people is not the restoration of God to its coinage, but to its life."

The attitudes of editorials in both the daily newspapers and the religious periodicals actually had little to do with the coin design. Upon close examination it became obvious that the critics were usually the same editors who had backed one of Roosevelt's opponents for the presidency. Those in favor of his election also supported his move to rid the coin of the motto. One hostile publication, the New York *Sun,* ran an anonymous poem in its edition of November 17, 1907. It read:

> In God We Trust
> Oh, no we don't
> That is, we mustn't say so;
> Such sentiment is out of date
> At least so says the potentate
> And He's the country and the State
>   Our Teddy.
> In God We Trust
> Upon Our Coins!
> Oh, sacrilegious people!
> God is not needed in this nation!
> We have the great Administration;
> And He's enough for all creation
>   Our Teddy.

Letters poured into the Capitol, and the issue of the motto became one for Congress to settle. It was obvious that the motto would have to be restored or the constituents would vote some of their representatives out of office. J. Hampton Moore, a Pennsylvania congressman, a Republican, and a close friend of Roosevelt, felt compelled to sponsor a bill to restore the motto. He explained to the President his feeling based on his interpretation of the public mood. Roosevelt then replied:

> The Congressman says the House Committee wants to pass a bill restoring the motto to the coin. I tell him it is not necessary; it is rot; but the Congressman says there is a misapprehension as to the religious purport of it—it is so easy to stir up a sensation and misconstrue the President's motives—and that the Committee is agitated as to the effect of a veto. I repeat, it is rot, pure rot; but I am telling the Congressman if Congress wants to pass a bill re-establishing the motto, I shall not veto it. You may as well know it in the Senate also.

On March 8, 1908, a bill authorizing the restoration of the motto "In God We Trust" on American coins passed the House, the Senate agreeing on May 13 of that year. Roosevelt, yielding to pressure, signed the bill into law five days after that. By July 1, all coins in production had the motto restored.

The Eagle

The use of the eagle as a symbol on coinage dates back to ancient times. It was a bird originally thought to be related to the god Jupiter, who used it to care for his lightning bolts. Coins struck to honor Jupiter frequently showed a stately eagle holding thunderbolts.

The eagle was an important part of ancient ritual. When an Emperor died and was laid upon a funeral pyre, an eagle was released from the flames so it would fly the Emperor's soul to heaven.

An example of what is know as a heraldic eagle as shown on the twenty-dollar gold piece.

A typical U.S. eagle design.

Some ancient coins feature the eagle standing between an owl and a peacock. The owl related to Minerva and the peacock to Juno. These goddesses were of great importance to the people, and numerous coins were struck with combinations of their symbols.

The Roman legions used the eagle as their primary standard. The birds were carved on top of spears, which were sharpened for sticking into the ground. They were also featured on coins, always with a thunderbolt clasped in their talons.

Benjamin Franklin was not particularly pleased with the idea of using an eagle on an American coin. He felt that the eagle was a filthy bird with no practical value to mankind. In a letter to his daughter, Mary Bache, he stated that he would prefer the turkey as a symbol for America. At least the turkey was both practical and a true native of the country.

Franklin's criticisms were scorned by other of the Founding Fathers. Judge Thatcher suggested, ". . . perhaps a goose might satisfy the gentleman better, as it was humble and re-publican enough, while the goslings would serve for the subsidiary pieces."

When coins first made their appearance in the United States, the eagle looked scrawny and pathetic. On April 5, 1792, a writer for the Newark *Gazette,* published in Newark, New Jersey, wrote:

Much time was spent in the House of Representatives on Saturday before they could agree on a proper device for the Federal coins. But instead of the emblematical figure of Liberty which they have adopted, how simple and apropos it would have been, since they have retained the Eagle on one side, to have placed fifteen emblematical pigeons on the other—a device which perhaps (all things considered) would be much more in character.

The Eagle, the arms of the U. States is a device of the old Congress; the symbol of office borne by the Serjeant at arms of the Present Congress has an Eagle on the top—so that it appears both old and new Congress had a latent design against the pigeons.

The most beautiful nineteenth-century use

of the eagle was on coins first released in 1836. The eagle was prepared by ornithological artist, Titian Peale, who was originally striving for the greatest possible realism. Although his preliminary sketches for the bird were exact, the final design adopted for the coinage was more symbolic than anatomically perfect.

For many years it was assumed that the model for Peale's eagle was an eagle that had adopted the U. S. Mint in Philadelphia for its home. The story of that bird was told in a copy of *Harper's Young People,* then quoted in one of the issues of the *American Journal of Numismatics* put out in 1893. That article stated:

On the Dollars of 1836, 1838 and 1839, and the nickel cents coined in 1856, is the portrait of an American eagle which was for many years a familiar sight in the streets of Philadelphia. "Peter" one of the finest eagles ever captured alive, was the pet of the Philadelphia Mint, and was generally known as the "Mint Bird." Not only did he have free access to every part of the Mint, going without hindrance into the treasure vaults, where even the treasurer of the United States would not go alone, but he used his own pleasure in going about the city, flying over the houses, sometimes perching upon lampposts in the streets. Everybody knew him, and even the street boys treated him with respect.

The Government provided his daily fare, and he was as much a part of the Mint establishment as the Superintendent or the Chief-coiner. He was kindly treated and had no fear of anybody or anything, and he might be in the Mint yet if he had not sat down to rest upon one of the great flywheels. The wheel started without warning, and Peter was caught in the machinery. One of his wings was broken, and he died a few days later. The Superintendent had his body beautifully mounted, with his wings spread to their fullest extent; and to this day Peter stands in a glass case in the Mint cabinet. A portrait of him as he stands in the case was put upon the coins named.

The reality of the coin design is somewhat different, however. Peale, like most artists capturing wildlife, killed his subjects, then stuffed and mounted them. Mint Director Robert Patterson touched on this fact in a letter to Treasury Secretary Levi Woodbury written April 9, 1836. He said, in part:

The die for the reverse is not yet commenced, but I send you the drawings which we propose to follow,—the pen sketch being that which we prefer. The drawing is true to nature, for it is taken from the eagle itself,— a bird, recently killed, having been prepared, and placed in the attitude which we had selected.

Today the eagle is required by law on our coins, though it almost disappeared from the reverse of the Franklin half dollar. The eagle was added as an afterthought since the omission violated the law. It is extremely tiny, to one side of the Liberty Bell.

The Figure of Liberty

The idea of Liberty, personified by a woman, is thought to be an American invention, since it has appeared since our earliest coins. However, it is a symbol that dates back to the ancients.

In ancient Rome, Libertas was the goddess of freedom, with her own temple located on the Aventine. She was a relatively minor figure among the deities and her early renderings show her as being quite different from the strong, wise gods who dominated Mount Olympus. Frequently she was shown as being a wealthy matron, bedecked with jewels. She seemed like a member of a first-night audience at the opera rather than a goddess with superhuman powers.

The concept of Libertas developed by the artists changed after the assassination of Julius Caesar. She had periodically been adorned with a veil, the symbol of divinity. However, after Caesar's death she was frequently portrayed as wearing a cap and holding a dagger. The conspirators chose this design to symbolize the idea that they had taken arms in violence against Caesar only to protect Rome from the late dictator's tyranny.

The cap that adorned Libertas was known as a pileus. It was made from wool and commonly worn by Roman laborers, fishermen, and other semiskilled workers. Most other Romans went about with their heads bare.

In the area of Phrygia, the wearing of the pileus was adopted by the owners of newly freed slaves who were placed for sale in the marketplace. These were "used" slaves about whom the sellers made no guarantees. The cap became the sign that the person was available "as is." It was an early form of "buyer beware."

Later the cap became a symbol of freedom. Instead of newly freed slaves in the marketplace wearing the pileus, it was worn by individuals who had won their freedom. This symbolic development is what caused its as-

sociation with the personified Liberty and was the reason it became the image of freedom.

By the time the new United States coins were developed, the country had endured tyranny under the British monarchy, violent revolution, and hard-won freedom. The use of Liberty adorned with a pileus became a popular design for early coins.

Examples of the head of Liberty as it has appeared over the past two hundred years.

Chapter 6

THOSE COINS YOU CAN NEVER OWN

One of the most interesting aspects of coin collecting is the topic of coins that are illegal to possess. These are coins that were legitimately created, then declared illegal for one reason or another. In the case of United States coins, the three most popularly discussed illegal issues are the 1933 gold twenty-dollar coin designed by Saint-Gaudens, the 1964 silver dollar, and the 1973 aluminum Lincoln cent.

On March 6, 1933, with President Franklin D. Roosevelt in office just two days, Proclamation 2039 was issued. It closed the banks throughout the country and declared that the hoarding of gold coins was no longer legal. Many people were hiding quantities of gold coins as a safety measure after their other investments, stocks usually bought on margin, became worthless or drastically dropped in value at the end of 1929. However, this hoarding of gold was being made illegal as a first step toward taking the United States completely off the gold standard.

In an 11-day period lasting from March 4 through March 15, 1933, $370 million in gold coins and paper money redeemable only in gold were returned to the Treasury. This was in line with the Secretary of the Treasury's order of March 6, which stopped all financial institutions from paying out gold or gold certificates and further eliminated the use of gold in commerce.

Despite what was happening with the banks and the withdrawal of gold, the Philadelphia Mint went ahead and began striking gold coins. By May 19, there were 445,500 $20 gold pieces dated 1933. These were intrinsically worth $20.67 each by then because of an increase in the valuation of gold, a fact that further led to their eventual disappearance.

While the gold coins were being struck, it was determined that the American dollar had to be devalued in light of the world gold prices. Toward this end, an order was issued on April 3 that required the public to return all their gold coins to the Federal Reserve banks. The exceptions were to be "rare and unusual" coins—collectors' items, actually—and common gold worth a maximum of one hundred dollars. Yet despite this order, the mint continued stamping twenty-dollar gold pieces.

According to U.S. coin laws dating back to

The 1913 Liberty-head nickel, its origin clouded in mystery, remains one of the most sought-after coins despite a value in excess of three hundred

thousand. Only five exist, and they were illegally made. However, they have not been confiscated, though their ownership is illegal.

the establishment of the U. S. Mint, a sampling of all gold and silver coins had to be checked by a presidential commission to determine that their content was correct. Twenty-nine of the 1933 twenty-dollar gold pieces were set aside for this purpose, the remainder of the run placed into the mint's vaults for safekeeping.

On May 1, 1933, all gold in the nation, with the exception of the coins retained under the rarity clause, were controlled by the government. This prepared the country for nationalization of the gold, a situation that was approved by Congress as part of the Gold Reserve Act of January 30, 1934. Gold was no longer a part of the American system of coinage, and the 1933-dated twenty-dollar gold pieces held in the vaults would not be released.

On Valentine's Day 1934, the presidential commission solemnly checked the twenty-nine gold coins set aside from the previous year's run. When this was over, they would theoretically be removed and melted.

What happened next is a mystery that has never been solved. There is a chance that some of the assay commissioners appointed by the President were responsible for stealing specimens of the 1933 gold coins. It is also possible that mint workers stole some of the coins from storage. They were checked by weight, and that weight was the same for earlier issues. It would have been a simple matter to remove some 1933-dated twenty-dollar gold coins and replace them with the same denomination of identical weight but from an earlier year's mint strikes.

After all the orders were issued to withdraw gold, melting of the stored gold coins began. The government found that gold storage could be more efficiently accomplished with multi-ounce gold bars than it could with millions of bagged coins.

The next few years remain a mystery in terms of the whereabouts of a small number of twenty-dollar gold coins dated 1933 that escaped the mint. Most likely they were held by collectors who took pleasure in owning an object no one else could obtain. They were not sold on the open market, and most collectors were unaware that they might exist.

In December of 1944, ten years after the twenty-dollar gold coins became illegal, the New York coin dealer Stack's sold the J. F. Bell collection of gold coins. It was the most comprehensive collection of gold ever assembled at that time, including all U.S. issues as well as those privately issued coins used to alleviate coin shortages in San Francisco and other early boom towns. Yet despite the completeness, there were a few varieties not included. One was the 1933 coin, listed as having been privately sold for one thousand dollars—a major figure for those days.

In July of 1947, the government discovered that a man named L. G. Barnard was in possession of a 1933-dated twenty-dollar gold piece. The United States Western District Court of Tennessee was the scene of the action, and Barnard had little hope of winning. His only defense was that the coin was rare and unusual, criteria President Roosevelt had used when telling the public which coins they could keep. This was of little value since that order was meant for all legally issued gold pieces and not for a coin that never should have left the mint.

Judge Boyd ruled against Barnard. He said, in part: "It is the court's opinion this coin was abstracted by someone who had in mind that it would have a special value as a rare and unusual coin and that it could be disposed of from that standpoint."

The judge then went on to explain why the 1933 coin did not fit the Roosevelt definition of rare and unusual. He said: "It is a fair inference that the double eagle here involved was taken out of the mint in an unlawful manner; and, further, it is entirely reasonable to say, considering the customs and strict practices at the mint, that it was abstracted by someone who substituted a similar coin for it before the coins were reduced to bullion." The coin was returned to the government.

In 1954, the Egyptian Government held an auction of the coins belonging to the deposed King Farouk. Included in the collection was a 1933 U.S. twenty-dollar gold coin.

Word of the Farouk coin reached the United States Government, which brought diplomatic pressure to bear to have it returned. The Egyptian Government agreed to withdraw the coin from sale but did not return it. Whether it still holds it or it was sold to a collector is not known. So long as it is not in the United States or held by a United States citizen, there is nothing the U. S. Government can do to regain the specimen. The value to collectors would be high, since it is the only specimen available. Even in Europe, where U.S. coin collecting is not so popular, a figure of from $250,000 to $500,000 for the coin would not be out of line.

The only other known specimens of the 1933 twenty-dollar gold piece are in the Smithsonian Institution collection and will never be sold. There they remain for everyone to enjoy.

The 1964 silver dollar is America's mystery coin. Officially it does not exist. Unofficially there have been reports of a specimen or specimens held by collectors who are hoping that one day the coin or coins can legally be sold.

In August of 1964, Congress authorized that forty-five million silver dollars be struck and allocated six hundred thousand dollars toward this end. The coins would bear the same peace design found on the 1921 and later issues. They would be used to meet the needs of businesses, primarily the gambling interests in Nevada.

The production of the silver dollars was probably an example of Congress yielding to special interests. A serious shortage of smaller-denomination coins existed, and silver stockpiles were decreasing rapidly. The new silver dollar was the last coin needed in production, and a few level heads in Congress managed to delay production for several months. However, on May 15, 1965, President Lyndon Johnson issued an order that started production. A total of 316,076 regular-issue pieces and 30 trial strikes were prepared at the Denver Mint. They were dated "1964" despite the fact that they were made the following year.

The United States Mint's officials were angered by having to produce the 1964 silver dollars. Instead of solving any shortage in the gaming industry, officials felt the coins would never reach circulation. Since these were the first silver dollars to be issued in 30 years, it was assumed that collectors would grab them all. This belief was enhanced by the fact that coin dealers were already advertising their interest in buying them, offering as much as $7.50 each!

The mint officials managed to convince enough congressmen of the folly of releasing the silver dollars to get the production stopped. Furthermore, all the coins that had been produced were to be melted with the exception of two of the trial strikes. These trial strikes were sent to Washington for careful study and analysis, then melted in 1970.

The problem with the 1964 silver dollars is that it is believed that not all the coins were melted. A dishonest mint worker could have exchanged one or more coins for older silver dollars of similar design. In fact, there are a number of reports that at least one genuine specimen is held by a collector, and these reports are considered reliable. However, they generated so much interest by the Treasury Department that whoever may have them has refused to come forward with pictures, the coin or coins, or other evidence. It would result in immediate prosecution.

If a 1964 silver dollar does exist, it is undoubtedly being held in the hope that the law will one day change and it will become legal to possess it. At that time, it will undoubtedly sell for a tremendous sum of money, especially if it is unique.

Of course, there could be a problem even if the coin is made legal. Since no other speci-

mens exist, including in the Smithsonian collection, there is no way to determine whether or not the dollar might be fake. A skilled counterfeiter could easily prepare what seems to be a 1964 silver dollar, and no one would know for certain if it is genuine. Thus the coin may always remain a mystery to collectors.

The story of the 1973 aluminum cent is a story of congressional scandal. Several of these coins exist illegally, stolen by congressional representatives and/or their staff members, and these thefts have never been solved.

The 1885 trade dollar is another illegal issue of the mint that is in private hands. Apparently mint workers made the coin from dies they designed themselves. Unlike earlier issues, there was no authorization for these dies. Their value has been estimated to be in excess of one-quarter million dollars today.

The story of the aluminum cent goes back to 1973, when the price for copper was rising to such a degree that the mint officials felt there would come a day when the cost of copper plus production would exceed the face value of the one-cent piece. It was decided to find an alternative material, much as silver coins had been changed to a clad cupro-nickel "sandwich."

On December 7, 1973, Treasury Secretary George P. Shultz prepared a bill for introduction in Congress. It stated, in part:

A BILL

To authorize the Secretary of the Treasury to change the alloy and weight of the one-cent piece.

Be it enacted by the Senate and House of Representatives of the United States of America in Congress assembled, That section 3515 of the Revised Statutes, as amended (31 U.S.C. 317), is further amended by designating the existing section as subsection (a) and by adding a new subsection (b) to read as follows:

(b) Whenever the Secretary of the Treasury determines that the use of copper in the one-cent piece is no longer practicable, he may change the alloy of the one-cent piece to not less than 96 per centum of aluminum and such other metals as he may determine. The one-cent piece authorized by this subsection shall have such weight as may be prescribed by the Secretary.

The bill immediately brought criticism from a number of areas. Senator Mark Hatfield of Oregon noted that aluminum was not only in short supply, it could also only be produced with methods using a great deal of energy. Since the nation was supposed to be conserving its energy, this fact seemed to make the proposition inappropriate.

The vending industry was opposed to aluminum after samples—blank aluminum pieces the exact size and weight of the cent to be produced—jammed vending machines during testing. As many as one in ten caused serious problems during the tests.

In the end, it was decided that aluminum cents would not be practical. The price of copper could rise at least to $1.50 a pound (It had reached just $1.00 a pound at its high

point) and still be practical for cent production. Furthermore, the complaints by vendors seemed to prove that the change was senseless. Thus the matter was ended. Or was it?

During the period of debate, aluminum cents were actually put into production by the mint. A total of 1.57 million pieces were prepared from Lincoln-cent dies dated 1974. They were going to be put into circulation as soon as Congress approved but, in the end, had to be melted.

In addition to the melted coins, five specimens of the aluminum cents were presented to the Senate Banking, Housing, and Urban Affairs Committee, and nine of the aluminum cents were given to the House Banking and Currency Committee. Most of these were not returned to the mint for melting. Instead, they seemed to "disappear" as congressional representatives, senators, and/or their staff members quietly pocketed what were instant rarities by virtue of the melting of the remaining coins. The mint officials had requested their return and explained how valuable they were when they first presented Congress with the coins for study.

In researching what was being done to retrieve the cents, I contacted the mint and received a letter from Acting Director Frank MacDonald, which stated in part:

You may be sure that appropriate steps are being taken to assure that the coins remain in the custody of the United States Government. Even while the proposed legislation was pending, all experimental aluminum pennies in Mint custody were ordered to be melted by the Director. The pieces provided the Committee remain in their custody and will presumably be returned to the Bureau once the Committees no longer have any need for them.

In other words, there was no crime. So long as the congressional committee retained them, they must have good and valid reason for doing so. At least that was the official comment.

The FBI was not in the same situation. Clarence Kelley, then the director, was in the process of investigating the missing cents, a fact made known to me by Senator Edward W. Brooke of Massachusetts. A letter from Director Kelley stated, in part:

The FBI was instructed by the Department of Justice to consult with officials of the Bureau of the Mint about the disappearance of several prototype aluminum pennies in order to determine if there was any violation of the Federal statute governing theft of Government property. This matter is currently under investigation and therefore facts of this case cannot be discussed.

When Director of the Mint Mary Brooks was asked about the FBI investigation, she referred me to MacDonald's letter, saying: "We have nothing further to add to our previous correspondence with you."

An attempt was made to reach every congressional committee member who had contact with the aluminum cents to see what they had to say. Many of the responses indicated ignorance of the situation. Others claimed the coins were taken back by the mint officials. For example, Clair W. Burgener, representative from California's Forty-second Congressional District at that time, said:

I was a member of the House Committee on Banking and Currency during the 93rd Congress, for the years 1973 and 1974. During that time I was indeed a member of the Subcommittee on Consumer Affairs which handled legislation relating to the minting of U.S. coins. I do recall that one day Mrs. Mary Brooks, Director of the Mint, showed members of the Committee the pattern aluminum cents which you referred to in your letter. I did have the opportunity to look at them, but I never had any of them in my personal possession. The ones that were shown that day, to the best of my recollection, were taken from the room by Mrs. Brooks.

There has been some debate about whether or not the various congressmen knew the aluminum cents were valuable. A number of the people in attendance when the coins were passed out claimed that nothing was said about their value. However, their statements became suspect when others, also present at the same time, made it clear they were alerted to the possible worth of the coins. As Representative Burgener said in that same letter:

I was told at the time that they had substantial value although, not being a coin collector or knowledgeable in the field, this meant little to me at the time.

Maine's Senator William D. Hathaway told me:

In the Fall of 1973 the Director of the Mint, Mary Brooks, visited my office and left with me one of the sample aluminum pennies. To the best of my recollection a few days later a representative from the Mint came by the office and picked up the sample coin.

John B. Conlan, an Arizona congressman, was upset when he saw the aluminum cents because he did not like the idea of having something with so little intrinsic worth. He told me:

I remember seeing the coins, handling them briefly and cursing them a bit. Beyond that, I don't have any idea what happened to them.

Some individuals were involved with the coinage law that would affect the aluminum cents but claimed to have nothing to do with the coins themselves. Senator William E. Brock III of Tennessee said:

My records indicate that the date the Senate Committee on Banking, Housing and Urban Affairs considered the legislation to provide for the composition change was December 13, 1973. At this meeting of the full committee, which was to resume the markup of the bill that eventually became the Housing and Community Development Act of 1974, Senator Sparkman brought the Administration's request to our attention. I recall, there was no extended debate, only a brief explanation of the bill, before the Committee approved the measure by voice vote. To my knowledge, there were no representatives of the Bureau of the Mint or the Department of the Treasury present and no "samples" available.

One congressional comment came not from a person who was involved but from Senator Barry Goldwater of Arizona, who had nothing to do with the situation. He wrote as a favor to Senator Robert Taft, Jr., of Ohio, who admitted to having had two of the cents at one time, according to an article in the *Wall Street Journal,* then losing them. Goldwater wrote:

> In speaking with an official at the Bureau of the Mint I was advised of the following:
>
> 1. The aluminum coins were formulated as a possible substitute to the copper pennies presently in use. This plan arose out of the copper shortage which was prevalent in 1973.
> 2. Aluminum coins were worked up and sent to the House and Senate Banking Committees for investigation. However, while investigations were being conducted, the copper shortage eased and it was decided to forgo plans for aluminum pennies.
> 3. At no time did the Bureau of the Mint ask for the return of the samples sent to the Congressional Committees and they feel there is no evidence of wrongdoing on anyone's part.

It is interesting to note that after a number of investigations by various writers, including myself, a few of the coins were discovered. A former secretary for one of the members of the Banking Committee happened to find two of the cents in her home. Although she knew not how they got there, she had the presence of mind to mail them back to the mint officials.

A member of Congress also "found" one of the coins. It was in an office ashtray and returned.

The only congressional staff member who ever admitted to deliberately holding onto one of the aluminum cents was Charles B. Holstein, a former professional staff member of the House Banking and Currency Subcommittee on Consumer Affairs. However, he apparently did not feel he had done anything dishonest. In April of 1975, Holstein announced that he had turned an aluminum cent over to the Smithsonian Institution for special display. He was quoted by David Ganz in an article in the newspaper *Coin World* as saying:

> For more than six months I kept the aluminum "penny" in my wallet. Mostly as a conversation piece, and as a reminder of the historical process that the subcommittee was deliberating on.

Apparently Holstein had first made contact with mint officials and was told that the cent, when returned, would be destroyed. He felt that by giving it to the Smithsonian, the coin curiosity would be preserved for future generations. The Smithsonian already possessed the 1933 twenty-dollar gold piece, and that coin, theoretically, should have been melted. He felt it was unlikely the aluminum cent would be destroyed with the action he took.

At this writing the remaining coins are still at large. It seems likely that they are in the possession of one or more individuals waiting for the controversy to die down so they can be quietly sold either openly or to someone for whom possession is more important than legality. The Treasury Department has told me that their investigators continue to be alert to coin auctions and advertisements that might indicate an aluminum cent is being sold. Should they discover one, it will be confiscated immediately. After that, whatever criminal prosecution is deemed appropriate will be made.

A check with coin dealers reveals that none

have been offered to the major retailers in the field. Benjamin Stack of New York's Stack's, Inc., summed up the general feeling about the matter when he said:

We, at Stack's, have never been offered any of these "infamous" aluminum cents, nor have we ever heard of anyone that has.

Further, we would NOT hesitate to have the individual prosecuted who might offer these "missing" coins into the market.

Frankly, from the news accounts we read, we doubt if any truth exists to the entire matter. If the story is fact, a member of Congress would have to be a damn fool to offer them to the numismatic fraternity. It would be my pleasure to expose him! The publicity would be worth a good deal more than the value of an unauthorized coin.

Chapter 7

COLLECTING "OTHER" MONEY

Some coin collectors shun coins entirely, preferring to acquire a different form of "money" as part of their hobby. They collect the barter objects that have frequently taken the place of coins over the years. A number of these have been mentioned in previous chapters. However, since "odd and curious" coins or "coin substitutes," as these objects are known, have been growing in popularity in recent years, it is worth looking at this field in a little greater depth.

In Asia, tea leaves served as a means of making payment for various goods and services. The leaves were pressed together into bricks, which often weighed several pounds. These were carefully weighed, then stamped with official symbols that gave them legal credibility as money.

Tea-leaf money was most popular in areas where vegetables and herbs either could not be readily grown or were in short supply. The bricks had value, not only because they were used as money but also because they could be dropped into water and made into a beverage the people could seldom get in any other way.

One type of coin substitute that is *not* likely to find its way into an odd and curious collection is a man's wife. At one time, men in parts of Africa collected wives as symbols of wealth. These women were not slaves, and this had nothing to do with the slave trade. However, when a man married, his wife became his "property" and could be traded for goods and services.

Tobacco was a popular form of money in the Maryland and Virginia colonies as well as in England. When a man married a girl who had to be brought to the colony from England, the captain of the ship transporting the bride-to-be to the colony would charge between 100 and 150 pounds of tobacco for his service.

Iron hoes were money substitutes in parts of Africa. The farmers valued them because they were so good for tilling the soil. In nonagricultural areas where the metal was scarce, the hoes were valued because they could be altered into weapons. The metals native to those areas were seldom as strong as the iron, so the hoes were quite valuable.

Slang terms for money have come from the use of various substitutes. For example, the skin of a male deer was worth a dollar, and thus the evolution of the term "one buck."

The Mayans made beads from green stones such as jade and jadite. The beads were holed, polished, then used singly or strung together as a form of currency.

In the early 1840s one money substitute was the cleanest form of cash you could get. Soap cakes were used in various Mexican towns, each cake valued at 1½ cents. The cakes of soap were stamped with the name of the town and the authorized manufacturer. The stamping was deep enough into the surface of the soap so that the bars could be used for washing. So long as the stamp was legible, it didn't matter how well used the soap might be, it would still be legal tender at full value.

Most people know about wooden nickels made as souvenirs for various events and promotions, but there was a period when coins were made from paper and circulated at full face value. This occurred in the area known as Leyden, which was under siege by the Spanish in the year 1574. Metal had become extremely scarce and coins were needed to insure normal commerce within the embattled town as well as for paying the soldiers defending it.

The answer to the coin shortage for the people of Leyden was to make paper coins. Each coin was basically cardboard, though the origin of the material is uncertain. It was either taken from the wood covers of religious books in the cathedral, or the pages of religious books were glued together to form the crude cardboard. Whatever the case, the paper coins were then stamped from the same dies that would have been used to make regular coinage had metal been available.

After World War I, the German mark depreciated in value to such a degree that it was no longer practical to make such coins in any metal other than copper or iron. Since copper and iron were in short supply, the German Government went to a porcelain factory in Meissen and had coins produced from that material. Actually this was not an original idea. The same plant had been used to pro-

duce a series of porcelain coins for Germany back at the end of the eighteenth century.

It took a wheelbarrow to handle the giant copper plates coined by King Frederick I of Sweden back in 1731. A ten-daler copper plate weighed forty-eight pounds, and an eight-daler plate weighed thirty-two pounds. The most common giant copper, the four-daler plate, still weighed six pounds, much too heavy to carry in one's pocket. These copper plates were valued in relation to silver, which was a much more valuable metal, ounce for ounce, thus forcing the larger size.

Since the people couldn't easily carry the copper-plate money, they wheeled it to the Bank of Sweden for safekeeping. Then they were given paper money whose face value was equal to the amount of copper-plate money on deposit. This paper money could be spent the same way as "hard" money because the people knew it was being issued in a quantity matching the private holdings of copper plates.

Walrus skins served as money for the Russians during the years 1818 through 1825 when the Russian-American Company explored the Aleutian Islands and the land along the northwestern coast of North America. These skins, which were made into fifty-kopeck notes, were actually being recycled after serving as a storage vessel.

The men who worked for the Russian-American Company had little interest in the walrus. The otter was their prey because the otter skins were so valuable. Each otter skin sold for ten rubles (two dollars), a substantial sum in those days. However, the otter skins had to be shipped, and the waterproof walrus hide seemed the ideal protection for wrapping rolled otter pelts.

Once the furs arrived at their destination, the walrus skins were recycled. Some were sewn together and used to cover chests of tea and other goods purchased in the Orient in exchange for the otter. The remainder were cut and stamped into currency valued at fifty kopecks each.

Nails once were valued as money. Each nail was handmade and valued according to such factors as the size and work involved in making it. The term "tenpenny nail" referred to the value of a nail of standard size, a term that has survived to this day, though the price per nail is no longer ten pennies.

Because nails were so expensive, colonial Americans who used them to build their cabins found that the cost of the nails was greater than the value of the cabin. In Virginia, for example, the colonists got into the habit of burning their cabins when they moved, thus freeing the nails, which would survive the fire undamaged. The nails were then taken to the next homesite and used for the new house. This produced a housing shortage, however, and the Virginia colonial government began paying the colonists the value of the nails in a cabin so it would not be destroyed.

California's Yurok Indians utilized woodpecker scalps for ornamental decoration. These were so important that certain values were assigned according to the size and quality of the scalp. The values generally ranged from fifty cents to five dollars. However, these figures were not consistent from tribe to tribe. The Hupa Indians of that state placed values of just ten cents to one dollar on the same range of scalps.

Sometimes odd and curious money is valued according to the ease with which it is found. The wapiti, an animal often mistakenly called an "elk," has only two canine teeth in its mouth. These were extracted by the Indians in areas such as Idaho, Montana, and Missouri. Each tooth was valued at twenty-five cents, and they were sewn onto women's clothing as a way of showing wealth. The Crow Indians would pay one hundred teeth for a good horse,

and one of their wealthy women might walk around with a dress valued at ten such horses.

The British treasury used tally sticks as a form of money during medieval days. Hazel and willow sticks were notched when you delivered money to the treasury. The notches indicated the size of the deposit and were meant as a form of receipt. Each stick was carefully split through special indentations, one side being retained by treasury officials and the other piece going to the depositor. The date of the transaction also went on the stick, a combination of clerical Latin and Norman French utilized for this purpose.

The tally sticks were supposed to be records but, since they indicated a set amount of money on deposit, they became a form of currency. People exchanged the tally sticks during business transactions, so the person eventually claiming the money the sticks represented might be far removed from the individual who originally made the deposit.

When George III came to power, he disliked the tally currency. He abolished it, ordering the tally sticks to be burned to heat the Parliament Building. The sticks were exceedingly dry from the type of use they had received, and the fire was hotter than would have been the case with wetter, fresh wood. The intensity of the heat caused the building to burst into flames. It was destroyed.

There are numerous other examples of odd and curious money. Many larger coin dealers have a few of these pieces in their stock, and others sell them through their auctions. Usually these are extremely inexpensive and are easier to store than metal coins, which can be damaged by exposure to the elements. They make an interesting aspect to a regular coin collection as well as an unusual hobby by themselves.

Chapter 8

PRIVATE MINT ISSUES

Anyone who has read a Sunday supplement in recent years is aware of the tremendous number of private mints offering coins, medals, ingots, and numerous other items. These are limited editions, generally made from high-grade precious metal and undeniably beautiful. But exactly what are they? How do they fit into a coin collection? And what is their future resale potential?

To understand how the private mints came about, it is necessary to look back to the state of coin collecting in the early 1960s. During that period, the hobby suddenly went insane. Instead of a few thousand individuals quietly buying, trading, and selling their coins, it seemed like everyone was checking their pocket change and buying anything an "expert" said would make them rich.

The early 1960s was a period of insane speculation. The 1960 Lincoln cents were discovered to have a die variety so that some of the coins had a small zero in the date and others had a large zero. The small date was relatively common in terms of number made but scarcer than the cents with the larger date. Thus people began buying countless rolls of the small-date coins, certain they would get rich. They never considered the fact that the existence of so many rolls of these coins in the first place indicated they were too common to ever be very valuable.

Suddenly the prices rose to dizzying heights. At one convention I attended, the small-date Lincoln cents made in Denver were selling for $2.50 per uncirculated roll of 50 coins on Friday, the first day of convention. People attending the convention bought every roll they cou'd find and, by the time selling stopped on Friday night, the rolls were going for $3.50.

The next morning, Saturday, rolls of the 1960-D (Denver) small-date Lincoln cents were selling for $5.00, and by late afternoon the coins were going for just under $7.50 a roll. What had happened was that dealers brought a relatively limited number of coins to the convention and they had quickly sold out. There was no way to replenish their supplies through normal channels, so they had to buy rolls back from collectors attending the convention in order to resell the same rolls to collectors who had yet to get involved with this great "bargain." They bought and sold the same rolls of coins many times over, usually at increasingly higher prices.

Sunday at noon marked the last day of the convention, and everyone attending wanted to go home a "winner." They began dumping their rolls, hoping to sell out, make a quick "killing" and go home with considerably more money than they had when they came. The idea didn't work.

As soon as everyone began dumping their rolls of Lincoln cents, there was no longer a shortage. Dealers were faced with going home with just as many rolls as they had brought when they came. They also knew that there was no one to whom they might sell the coins except their regular customers who would be coming to their shops the following week, and those customers wouldn't pay inflated prices. As a result, the dealers offered sellers less money than the price of the coins when the show first opened. Everyone selling on Sunday took a substantial loss. Others decided to take their inflated small-date cents home for safekeeping to wait until the price skyrocketed again. Unfortunately the coins did not rise as anticipated, and the buyers lost money in the long run as well.

Even scarce coins were manipulated in the 1960s. The 1909 Lincoln cents containing the designer's initials—V.D.B.—and minted in San Francisco (1909-S V.D.B. is the way collectors designate it) is genuinely scarce in uncirculated condition. At this writing it sells for over $300, and that price is probably realistic for today's market. However, this same coin sold for more money in the 1960s than it does now.

The reason for the 1909-S V.D.B.'s radical change in value is that wealthy speculators managed to buy enough of the coins to deplete the market. This manipulation drove up the price dealers were willing to pay until it reached a point high enough that the speculators chose to unload. Then the market was flooded and the value dropped. Supply caught up with demand.

The 1909-S V.D.B. Lincoln cent.

This same speculation occurred with other American coins as well. Roosevelt dimes, Jefferson nickels, and Washington quarters that had certain dates were among denominations artificially manipulated by individuals with big bankrolls and a gambling instinct. Prices went crazy.

The situation was not true with the great rarities—coins so scarce that it would be almost impossible to corner the market by buying them all. These continued to rise at a steady rate, generally 10 per cent to 15 per cent per year, and remained just as good investments as they have always been. The problem was only with the more common material.

It soon became obvious that not only was coin collecting becoming a major hobby in terms of numbers of participants, but also the people entering collecting for the first time would buy anything that sounded potentially profitable. Thus the market was ripe for a new type of business devoted to collectors seeking both beauty and a cash return on their purchases. The age of the private mint was about to begin.

Medals have long been a part of our heritage. For centuries, these generally circular, beautifully designed objects have been produced to denote acts of valor, commemorate a special event, or commemorate a person of notable achievement. The United States Mint struck medals at the time of the signing of the many Indian peace treaties, for example. There were medals produced showing each of the U. S. Presidents. And even today, the U. S. Mint has a vast series of medals honoring our nation's heroes, all available to the public for a modest fee.

In addition to the official U. S. Government-produced medals, there have been a number of private companies producing medals on their own. These private medals were never merchandised very widely. Often they were available in unlimited quantity and had relatively few people collecting them. They were seldom seen as investments and most never rose in value beyond their issue price.

The "parent" of the private mints that took the production and promotion of medals to a new level of aggressiveness was Franklin Mint, now located in Franklin Center, Pennsylvania. This firm developed the mass-marketing techniques that included advertising in various publications such as Sunday magazine supplements of daily newspapers. Each advertisement offered a series of medals all based around a single theme. The medals were pure silver, for the most part, one ounce in weight, and beautifully designed. A strict cutoff date was given, and there was a promise that the number of medals produced would be limited to the number ordered by cutoff date. In addition, payment had to be made in advance. No medals were produced until the cash was in hand, so there was no chance of the company losing money by having overproduction.

The result of this plan was that the public had the opportunity to buy limited-edition silver medals with solid intrinsic worth and beautiful design. The items had scarcity, inner worth, and a desirable appearance. They proved the most popular numismatic items of their day—at least at first.

Before getting into the story of what happened to the private mint issues, let us look at the history of Franklin Mint, the first of the private mints to become a large-scale success. The mint's history goes back to 1959. That was the year a man named Joe Segel went into the medal business. Prior to that time, he had been involved with a number of different endeavors, none of which had proven very successful. He headed a merchandising gift club called Sales Promotion Industries, which was financially backed by Charles Andes and Norman Cohn, two close friends. They did not have enough money to adequately support expenses, and not even a Small Business Administration Loan was able to make them very solvent. The business was eventually sold to the Norman Cohn family.

Segel and Cohn remained friends, involving themselves in other business ventures, none of which proved very successful. However, in 1964, while watching television with Cohn, Segel had an idea that was to make him rich beyond his imagination.

In 1964 silver coins were withdrawn from

circulation, and Segel happened to be watching television the day before the law effecting that withdrawal went into effect. There was a news program being shown and it featured a story about the thousands of people lining up at the banks to buy silver dollars at face value while such purchases were still legal. It was a revelation to Segel. He knew there were coin collectors, but it was the film of thousands of them patiently waiting in line to buy coins that made him realize how big a business that could be. It was a market he felt should be tapped in some way.

The answer Segel decided upon was to create a series of commemorative medals. He felt that if the medals had intrinsic worth, memorialized a popular figure, and were properly merchandised, they could be extremely successful. General of the Army Douglas MacArthur, one of the nation's most popular war heroes, had recently died, so Segel decided a MacArthur commemorative would be the ideal first medal. And thus was the National Commemorative Society created.

Segel created several different categories for membership in his National Commemorative Society for fees ranging from $10 to $40. He advertised his newly created program in various trade journals, receiving 5,000 paid applications.

The early medals Segel produced were costly. Usually a silver medal sold for at least twice its intrinsic worth, and there was no real guarantee that the item would ever have greater value than its metal content. However, Segel was convinced that if the artistic design was of exceptionally high quality, the public would not be overly concerned about the final price. He constantly tried new coin-making equipment, striving to find the best the world had to offer. He also hired Gilroy Roberts, taking him from his job as chief engraver for the U. S. Mint, where Roberts had gained fame for his portrait of John F. Kennedy that appears on the popular fifty-cent piece.

The medal-making firm prospered and ex-panded, changing its name to General Numismatics Corporation. Segel and Roberts continued their efforts to produce the most perfect medallic art they could, developing new types of equipment of their own design. The firm also became the unofficial producer of medals for other organizations, such as Basco Jewelers, the Penn Central Railroad, and others.

In 1965, Segel decided he could maintain quality while expanding production. He looked around for a new market for his company's services and chanced upon Las Vegas. The clubs in Vegas were becoming desperate for a dollar-coin substitute after the withdrawal of silver dollars from circulation. They had maintained a large supply of silver dollars, but their hoard was dwindling rapidly.

Segel got together with club owners, U. S. Government officials, and others to determine what kind of gaming token was needed and how it could be prepared without being counter to coin laws. He soon developed a counter acceptable to everyone including casino security personnel and began producing them in large quantity. He continued this relationship for four years and it became a highly profitable aspect of his business.

The Franklin Mint evolved from these early companies of Segel. Mailing lists had been developed from various product lines and, in 1967, a Presidential Medal series featuring the portraits of the 36 Presidents brought in 3,600 prepaid subscriptions. Next came a series of 60 medals based on stories in the Bible. A total of 4,100 subscribers were interested in that.

Also in 1967 came a medal series that was one of the mint's most successful offerings. In honor of the American Bicentennial, 200 medals were to be struck honoring the history of the United States. Two medals a month would be released, the series not being completed until 1976. This was the most heavily promoted of all offerings, $350,000 being spent before anyone was certain it would succeed. However, orders came in bringing 100 times the advertising cost. Orders totaled $35 million, a sum so impressive that numerous other business people decided to take the plunge and form their own private mints to compete with Segel.

The new mints had such names as Hamilton Mint, George Washington Mint, Lincoln Mint, Mount Everest Mint, and Letcher Mint. Many utilized former Franklin Mint personnel, who were hired away or who left to found one of the new mints. Some innovated new ways of making medals, such as the Letcher Mint's creation of a gold-on-silver process that resulted in a two-tone, bimetallic medal.

To say that the early days of the private mints were successful is an understatement. Some of the executives lived like a sheik from one of the oil-rich countries. Segel, for example, owned a Pennsylvania mansion that included at least three telephones (rumors said twelve, but only three could be confirmed) in just one of the bathrooms. He traveled by chauffeured Lincoln Continental and had hideaways in the form of a condominium in Key Biscayne, Florida, and a ninety-room hotel in Switzerland.

The private mints went beyond the silver medals. They produced gold and bronze collectibles, silver one-ounce bars with special designs, and numerous other items. The Franklin Mint moved into the field of what are known as postal-numismatic covers, which are envelopes featuring commemorative stamps with either a coin or a medal attached, usually in a clear plastic window to the left side of the envelope. Some of these were prepared in conjunction with organizations such as Postmasters of America. Others were done with the assistance of a number of foreign countries.

Nonnumismatic items were added to the various Franklin Mint offerings and, to a lesser extent, the offerings of some of the competitors. For example, limited-printing first-edition books by famous authors, limited special printings of classic works bound in leather, sculpture in pewter and other materials, Christmas tree ornaments, and specially designed plates were among the many additional lines of collectibles.

The private mints became deeply involved with foreign countries whose governments were seeking ways to make money without being limited by their natural resources, manufacturing capacity, and similar restrictions. For years such countries, especially the Arab sheikdoms, had been utilizing their post offices for revenue. They would turn out all manner of stamps, including some made from gold foil, stamps with three-dimensional images and, in the case of the Asian country of Bhutan, a "stamp" that was actually a small record featuring the sounds of the country. There are far more stamps produced than the people can use. In fact, many of the countries have a population in large measure deprived of both the education to read and the income to send a letter. However, the postage stamps are sold to collectors who delight in the unusual, even when it is a matter of semantics whether or not the stamps are genuine postal issues.

The private mints convinced these countries that special-edition coins could generate as much money as the special stamps they were accustomed to offering. They decided to offer proof and uncirculated coins both individually and in sets. The coins would be produced by the private mints and officially made legal tender. However, they would not be produced in a quantity needed for domestic purposes—often an amount so small as to be meaningless. Rather, they would be offered to collectors at healthy premiums. Thus, though legal tender, they would probably never be spent. They were given the name noncirculating legal tender (NCLT) by the collectors who either purchased or cursed them. Their full story was told in Chapter 4.

There are times when the NCLT is so spurious that even the issuing country is in question. For example, there was a 1973 issue of coins for the Republic of Minerva produced by the Letcher Mint. This time the authorizing government did not really exist, at least not in a form that would win United Nations recognition. Quoting from the sales literature:

Hardly more than one year old, the Republic of Minerva is situated 400 miles south of Fiji at 23 degrees 40′ South Latitude and 179 degrees West Longitude. This "Free Enterprise" state is set up as a constitutional republic where government is limited to protection of its citizens against force and fraud, and cannot engage in commercial activities. Prior to its occupation on January 19, 1972, North and South Minerva Reefs were below sea level at high tide and remained unclaimed by any nation.

Thus we have a country that spent most of its time underwater. Perhaps Neptune could have needed coinage, though unless there are undersea cities it is hard to imagine a need for legal tender, circulating or not. However, the advertisement continued:

The founders of the present government carried out a land fill project to raise parts of the two reefs above high tide and in accordance with International Law proclaimed a new and independent nation.

The material discussed the fact that thirty thousand people would eventually live on the republic, though there was no mention of where they would be found or what might attract them to an area that just might be eroded back into the sea.

Next comes the rather unusual part of this country/noncountry's history. The sales literature stated:

During 1972 Minerva was forcibly invaded by the King of Tonga. The Minervians have been forced to set up a government in exile until the conflict is settled. The government, in cooperation with the Minerva Development Bank, Ltd., has authorized the striking and distribution of this limited edition of Gold

Relief $35 denomination coins to be sold at their face value by the Letcher Mint, the West's largest private mint.

Even the price of the Minerva "coin" seems a little silly. How many times have you had need for a thirty-five-dollar coin? For that matter, how many purchases are the people of this once-underwater, occupied "nation" going to make with this denomination? Yet it is legal tender. Or it will be. Or . . .

But despite the absurdity of some of the coins, the popularity of the private mint items was enormous. The Minerva coins probably did not sell all that well, though the NCLT of other nations certainly did. Many millions of dollars were spent by the general public on previous metal coins, medals, and similar items.

Part of the appeal was beauty. Another factor was the unusual quality of both the designs and the strikings compared with the lesser quality of American circulating issues. However, the largest appeal was the potential for investment, since these were usually limited offerings with small production quotas. Many people put their investment money into private mint issues rather than stocks or bonds, certain they would make more money. And, at first, the advertising for many of the private mint issues encouraged this belief. It was only when a few of the advertisements were considered to be in possible violation of truth-in-advertising regulations that the suggestion of potential profit was eliminated.

Within five years after the private mint offerings became popular, a number of collectors who had purchased the medals, ingots, and other items put their holdings on the open market. They were convinced that they would at least double their investment during resale and were shocked to find that there were no buyers anxious for what they owned. The dealers offered them just the intrinsic worth, which meant that many buyers had to take a 50 per cent loss on their investment.

Word about the lack of a secondary market for private mint issues spread quickly. Some collectors flooded the market, hoping to get whatever money they could. Others left their items in safe-deposit boxes, planning to give them to their children or grandchildren in the years ahead, hoping that in another generation the medals would have genuine value. Everyone warned their friends about the problems, and buying dropped rapidly. The mints had to face serious losses of revenue, and the majority of them either laid off some of their employees or added other lines of business.

Today the older offerings from private mints are readily available from a number of larger coin dealers who advertise regularly in the various hobby publications. The prices they charge for what are undeniably beautiful works of medallic art vary quite widely—from intrinsic worth to a figure perhaps 25 per cent to 50 per cent higher than intrinsic value—though almost all sell below issue price. Some of the dealers are trying to encourage such purchases in the hope of building a genuine secondary market for these collectibles. However, the results of their efforts will not be known for several years to come. The items may prove to be a passing fad that eventually get melted and sold for bullion, or they may be popular collectibles in the future.

Should you consider collecting private mint items? Certainly, even though most have no connection with coinage as such. They are among the finest examples of medallic art you can find, and their secondary-market selling price is reasonable. For example, a 12-medal series called Rockwell's Tribute to Robert Frost is beautifully designed and executed with the low mintage of just 12,544. The medals sold for $300 when issued and are available at this writing for $165 from one dealer and $195 from another, the price reflecting either the difference in area demand or a variance in the profit margins the dealers desire.

A 60 proof-medal series in silver depicted aspects of the creations of artist Michelangelo. It sold for $600 and generally is available for $400 at this writing.

Other series of medals offer similar savings. The same is true with many of the non-circulating legal-tender coins the private mints have produced.

There is also a catalog of retail prices for the most popular private mint issues, those made by the Franklin Mint. The catalog, *Guidebook of Franklin Mint Issues* by Chester Krause, is published by Krause Publications and is carried by many coin dealers. It offers a way of determining the value of different items and, if there ever is a large market for the medals, this catalog will help you judge price changes over the years. Since it is annually updated, it is an excellent reference.

Private mint issues are a highly debatable aspect of coin collecting. However, if you like them and recognize you'll never get rich from them, they can be an enjoyable collecting specialty by themselves or with your coin collection. Just be certain you compare dealer prices for the various items, as asking prices for the same items vary greatly around the country.

Chapter 9

COIN INVESTING

Collecting coins can be more than a hobby. It can also be a means of improving your financial future. The rarities of the world increase in value to such a degree that a common investment return is 15 per cent per year over the long term (five-year minimum holding time). Undoubtedly, as your collection grows, you may want to put a portion of your hobby money into one or more items meant strictly for investment. But which coins should you buy? And how do you avoid the risk of losing your money?

The value of a coin is based on two factors, both of which must always be present for a coin to be a good investment. These factors are rarity and demand. If there are only twenty-five examples of a particular coin in existence, it is undeniably rare. However, if only twenty-three people in the world are interested in buying it, there will be more coins than buyers. Anyone who wants one can offer very little money for the rarity, secure in the knowledge that if the seller refuses his offer, he can buy the coin elsewhere. The potential seller also knows this and is forced to agree to the low bid unless he or she wants to be stuck with that coin.

If there are twenty-five coins of a particular type in existence and one hundred people want them, there is far greater demand than there are existing pieces. When one is offered for sale, as many as seventy-five people may bid against one another for the chance to own it. The price rises steadily, each sale tending to bring in more money than the last. The value skyrockets and the coin proves to be a good investment.

At times the price for scarce coins is altered by manipulators who try to corner the market, then sell when the price rises. This has never happened with true rarities but there are some scarce, fairly expensive coins that have experienced this problem. For example, in the early 1960s, speculation was rampant. People would buy rolls of coins, put them away, drive up the prices, then dump them on the market. Some people made a lot of money. Most lost their "investment."

A good example of what speculation can do to a coin is the history of the 1909 Lincoln

When the mints goof, collectors benefit. Mint error collecting is becoming big business. Many collectors are investing in this field, and there are a number of guide books available. It remains highly speculative, but the coins are among the most interesting you can get. Shown is a Lincoln cent struck off center. Most of the planchet is blank.

cent made in the San Francisco Mint and bearing the initials V.D.B. The initials stood for the designer's name—Victor David Brenner.

In 1958, the uncirculated 1909-S V.D.B. Lincoln Cent, as it is known to collectors, sold for $65. By 1960 its value had risen to $97.50, and speculators moved in. By 1965 the coin cost $350, and the speculators began selling their holdings. The year 1966 saw the coin go to $300, then continue to decline to a figure of $220 in 1969. At this writing, an uncirculated specimen can be purchased for around $300—less than in 1965.

How can you avoid falling victim to the speculators? Easy. There is a standard guide to the price of United States coins that is annually updated. This is *A Guide Book of United States Coins* by R. S. Yeoman, and it is available through every coin dealer in the

country. Collectors call it the "red book" and it lists the retail market value of all United States coins.

Red books have been issued since the late 1940s, well before the speculative era of the 1960s. If you are thinking of buying a particular coin for investment, go back through the red books to see what the yearly gain has been. Any coin that has risen steadily without showing the roller-coaster fluctuations caused by speculators is a potentially sound investment. There is no reason why a coin's value should not increase steadily over the years, never showing unusual dips and rises, and not continue the same way.

Remember that coins are not like other traditional investments. If you invest in stock, the value of the company can be destroyed by a major fire, embezzlement, rival product, or any other unpredictable calamity. If you invest in land, you must sell it to buyers who are interested in that particular property. If your land is in Oregon and buyers want land in Iowa, you can't move your holdings. Coins are not influenced by anything other than the marketplace, and they can be mailed anywhere in the world a buyer happens to be located.

Interest in coins varies each year. At this writing, silver dollars are extremely popular. In other years, quarters have generated great interest. At such times, the value of rarities tends to rise faster than usual, then levels off (but does *not* go down, as with speculation) when interest is elsewhere, rising again a few months later. Since coins held for investment should be kept for the long haul—2½ to 5 years minimum—this periodic price stabilization will not affect your total investment growth.

Where can you get hold of back issues of the red book? Many libraries have them either in the circulating section or in reference. If yours is not among them, the library of the American Numismatic Association is open to the general membership. You can request that the books be sent to you, paying postage and insurance both ways, or you can pay to have Xerox copies of the necessary pages made and mailed to you. It takes a little time but it pays off in "sure thing" investments. Membership information concerning the ANA is found later in this book.

Coins bought for investment should be the finest possible. They should be free from dam-

A pattern is a coin design that was tried and then rejected. Patterns often exist in quantities of less than a dozen yet can sell for well under a thousand dollars despite the great rarity. This is primarily because there have been few collectors in the past. Recently new guide books relating to patterns have been introduced, and more and more collectors are bidding on these items. Coins purchased today for a few hundred dollars, or a thousand at most, should climb steadily in the years ahead. The coin shown is an 1851 ring cent, one of many ways created to alter the value of coins without altering size or metal content. At this time, only the large cents were being issued, and it was discovered that copper within the coin would soon be worth more than the coin itself, and an alternative had to be found. Eventually the small-cent coin with the flying-eagle design the size of the current Lincoln cent was developed to take its place. However, prior to that, this pattern was tried by the mint.

age of any kind, never circulated, and, most important, well made. Although the pressure used to strike a coin is theoretically consistent from piece to piece, some coins leave the mint better struck than others. Flawless, well-struck coins are called "gems" by collectors and generally cost more. In fact, their resale value can be as much as 400 per cent more than an uncirculated coin that is not in such top condition.

What should you expect to pay for an investment-quality coin? Surprisingly little in some cases. Remember that a coin is not a good investment just because it is expensive. It is a good investment because the value has risen steadily year after year with no periods of speculation. Thus a 1904 silver dollar struck by the New Orleans Mint is an excellent investment in top condition at approximately $15 at this writing. Why do I say that? Ten years earlier the coin sold for $3.50 and it was never speculated.

A more expensive, quality-investment coin is the uncirculated, well-struck 1885 silver dollar made by the San Francisco Mint. At this writing, the coin sells for $115. That represents 1,000 per cent gain in the past 14 years. Twenty years ago the coin would have sold for just 2½ times face value!

Coin investing is best done with coins of the country in which you live. American coins sell best within the United States. British rarities only command top dollar in Britain. And the same is true with coins of other countries as well.

Coins costing $500 or less will, in general, rise faster than coins whose value exceeds $1,000. This is because there are far more collectors able to afford one or more rarities costing a maximum of a few hundred dollars than there are those who can swing the $1,000-and-up figures.

Coins meant for investment should always be stored in holders that protect them from damage, then placed in safe-deposit boxes at your bank. The holders, usually made from plastic, are chemically inert and only cost a few cents apiece for the least expensive ones. They are readily available from most coin dealers.

Copper coins are best avoided for investment purposes even though a number of cents and half cents have done extremely well over the years. The reason for this is that copper can be damaged just resting in the safe-deposit box. Factors such as humidity create havoc with copper, and many copper coins develop what is known as carbon spotting. This greatly diminishes the resale value of the coin. Such a problem is minor for the collector but a serious consideration for the person trying to increase wealth through the value of investment holdings.

Counterfeiting is a serious problem with rare coins. Such counterfeiting ranges from cementing a mint mark onto a coin because the genuine coin rarity has the mint mark, to actually casting a coin in its entirety. In theory, going to a legitimate dealer insures honesty. In reality, counterfeits can be more sophisticated than many dealers can detect, no matter how honest and well-meaning they may be. Fortunately there are services that authenticate coins. One is run by the American Numismatic Association. Another is run by the Professional Numismatists' Guild. Addresses for such services and information on how to use them are in a later section of this book. The cost is a flat fee or a percentage of the value, whichever is higher. On more expensive coins, certification costs are usually paid by the dealer. If you must pay the cost, have the dealer send the coin to the service at his or her expense. If it is not genuine, the arrangement should be such that you pay nothing. When the coin is genuine, the cost of the certification is added to your bill. It is a small price to pay for the protection it affords.

A record should be kept of your coin-investment purchases and this record retained in a location separate from the coins, preferably in another safe-deposit box. This record should

This is another pattern coin. The coin was designed by the mint's engraver when looking for a new dollar-coin design that would be acceptable to the public.

describe the coins, their condition, the date the coins were purchased, and the price paid. When investment coins are resold, the government currently taxes the difference between the purchase price and the resale price as a capital gain. This tax is lower at this writing than the standard income tax and is a minor nuisance for investors. However, not paying it can result in various penalties.

It is a good idea to insure your coin collection even if it is stored in the bank. There have been enough bank vault break-ins in recent years so even safe-deposit boxes are not 100 per cent safe, though they are far more secure than your home, even when you have a home safe. Collector organizations such as the ANA offer group insurance plans that are often less expensive than those available through your regular insurance agent. Currently one such plan charges 1 per cent of the coins' value when they are stored in a bank, with higher rates for coins stored anywhere else.

Foreign coins, especially ancients, have also proven to be good investments. However, learning to identify the rarities and discovering where to get the best financial return can be far more difficult than with American coin investments. If you are interested in this aspect of investment, educate yourself with the materials listed at the end of this book before making any purchases. A beginner is most likely to be successful specializing in coins of the United States because all the records you need are readily obtainable through the ANA library, among other sources.

Coin investing can be an enjoyable and profitable aspect of your new hobby. By using caution, having the items authenticated, and relying upon the proven history of a coin rather than listening to a speculator or promoter, you can make far more money than from almost any other form of investment.

Chapter 10

BUYING AND SELLING COINS

There was a time when coin collecting was a simple process. Each day a typical collector would go through the pocket change accumulated by members of his or her family, searching for different dates and mint marks of the various denominations being collected. Every week or two the collector would supplement the coins by going to the bank for one or more rolls of cents, nickels, dimes, or whatever. These would be carefully searched, then the remainder returned to the bank in exchange for currency or additional coins. With patience and much searching, collectors entering the hobby as recently as 1960 could accumulate numerous coins dating back into the late 1800s. They might obtain *silver* dollars, not the clad variety of recent years, and, occasionally, an odd denomination such as a three-cent piece wedged into a roll of dimes.

Then came the 1960s and the announcement that silver would no longer be used in American coinage. The value of silver had reached a point where the intrinsic worth of a coin was greater than the face value. Even the most common silver coin was valued at from 2½ to 3 times face, and this led to

hoarding and melting. Such pieces quickly disappeared from circulation. Almost overnight it was impossible to obtain an extensive collection of silver coins from circulation. Collectors continued to study pocket change and bank rolls but they could no longer anticipate favorable results from their endeavors. Most found themselves limited to collecting the new clad coins, but the available varieties were so limited that they did not yield the same enjoyment.

Today, many new collectors still diligently search their pocket change but they also realize the need to look beyond that source for additions to their collection. A certain amount of buying and horse trading is essential. This is also true for better-condition coins. Thus let us look at some of these aspects of coin collecting to see what to buy, and how and where to obtain it.

The price you pay for a coin is determined by scarcity, demand, and wear. In the chapter on coin investing, the first two categories are stressed far more than wear or "condition." This is because there are times that a true rarity can be in terrible shape and remain in demand. If you had a chance to possess a 1913 Liberty-head nickel, you would be happy to own it regardless of whether it was a proof or had the date barely visible. Only 5 such coins are known to exist, and there will always be a strong market for one of those specimens, no matter what its appearance.

With common coins, condition becomes more important. All coins of a similar design wear in much the same manner. Thus it has been possible to create terms for the different stages of wear; terms that dealers and collectors can use to evaluate the coins they are receiving. These are not completely exact, unfortunately, so there have been three "standard" grading guides developed (see book list), each of which differs slightly from the other two. Many collectors buy all three in order to gain the best possible understanding of their coins.

This rather unusual and quite beautiful design was created by mint engraver William Barber. It is called the Amazonian design.

To give you an example of what all this means, I will quote from the newest grading manual called the *Official ANA Grading Standards for United States Coins,* which is

put out by the Whitman coin division of Western Publishing Company, Racine, Wisconsin, in co-operation with the American Numismatic Association. Since the Lincoln cent is perhaps the most widely collected American coin, I am quoting the description of how to grade it. The book states:

SMALL CENTS—LINCOLN 1909 TO DATE

MINT STATE Absolutely no trace of wear.

MS-70 UNCIRCULATED Perfect
A flawless coin exactly as it was minted, with no trace of wear or injury. Must have full mint luster and brilliance or light toning. Any unusual die or planchet traits must be described.

MS-65 UNCIRCULATED Choice
No trace of wear; nearly as perfect as MS-70 except for some small blemish. Has full mint luster but may be unevenly toned or lightly finger-marked. A few barely noticeable nicks or marks may be present.

MS-60 UNCIRCULATED Typical
A strictly uncirculated coin with no trace of wear, but with blemishes more obvious than for MS-65. May lack full mint luster, and surface may be dull or spotted.
  Check points for signs of abrasion: high points of cheek and jaw; tips of wheat stalks.

ABOUT UNCIRCULATED Small trace of wear visible on highest points.

AU-55 Choice
OBVERSE: Only a trace of wear shows on the highest point of the jaw.
REVERSE: A trace of wear shows on the top of wheat stalks.
  Almost all of the mint luster is still present.

AU-50 Typical
OBVERSE: Traces of wear show on the cheek and jaw.
REVERSE: Traces of wear show on the wheat stalks.

Three quarters of the mint luster is still present.

EXTREMELY FINE Very light wear on only the highest points.

EF-45 Choice
OBVERSE: Slight wear shows on hair above ear, on the cheek, and at the jaw.
REVERSE: High points of wheat stalks are lightly worn, but each line is clearly defined.
Half of the mint luster still shows.

EF-40 Typical
OBVERSE: Wear shows on hair above ear, on the cheek, and on the jaw.
REVERSE: High points of wheat stalks are worn, but each line is clearly defined.
Traces of mint luster still show.

VERY FINE Light to moderate even wear. All major features are sharp.

VF-30 Choice
OBVERSE: There are small flat spots of wear on cheek and jaw. Hair still shows details. Ear and bow tie slightly worn but show clearly.
REVERSE: Lines in wheat stalks are lightly worn but fully detailed.

VF-20 Typical
OBVERSE: Head shows considerable flatness. Nearly all the details still show in hair and on the face. Ear and bow tie worn but bold.
REVERSE: Lines in wheat stalks are worn but plain and without weak spots.

FINE Moderate to heavy even wear. Entire design clear and bold.

F-12 OBVERSE: Some details show in the hair. Cheek and jaw are worn nearly smooth. LIBERTY shows clearly with no letters missing. The ear and bow tie are visible.
REVERSE: Most details are visible in the stalks. Top wheat lines are worn but separated.

VERY GOOD Well worn. Design clear but flat and lacking details.

VG-8 OBVERSE: Outline of hair shows but most details are smooth. Cheek and jaw are smooth. More than half of bow tie is visible. Legend and date are clear.
REVERSE: Wheat shows some details and about half of the lines at the top.

GOOD Heavily worn. Design and legend visible but faint in spots.

G-4 OBVERSE: Entire design well worn with very little detail remaining. Legend and date are weak but visible.
REVERSE: Wheat is worn nearly flat but is completely outlined. Some grains are visible.

ABOUT GOOD Outlined design. Parts of date and legend worn smooth.

AB-3 OBVERSE: Head is outlined with nearly all details worn away. Legend and date readable but very weak and merging into rim.
REVERSE: Entire design partially worn away. Parts of wheat and motto merged with the wreath.

NOTE: The Memorial cents from 1959 to date can be graded by using the obverse descriptions.

The following characteristic traits will assist in grading but must not be confused with actual wear on the coins:

Matte proof cents of 1909 through 1916 are often spotted or stained.

Branch mint cents of the 1920s are usually not as sharply struck as later dates.

Many of the early dates of Lincoln cents are weakly struck either on the obverse or the reverse, especially the following dates: 1911-D, 1914-D, 1917-D, 1918-D, 1921, 1922-D, 1923, 1924, 1927-D, 1927-S, and 1929-D.

1922 "plain" is weakly struck at the head, has a small I and joined RT in LIBERTY. Sometimes the wheat heads are weak on the reverse.

1924-D usually has a weak mint mark.

1931-S is sometimes unevenly struck.

1936 proof cents: early strikes are less brilliant than those made later that year.

1955 doubled die: hair details are less sharp than most cents of the period.

You will notice that there are three grades of uncirculated coins. That might not make a great deal of sense. After all, an uncirculated coin is exactly what the name implies—a coin that has never circulated. It is free from wear and looks just as it did the day it was produced at the mint. Since the coins are mass-produced and the striking pressure is theoretically constant with modern machinery, how can there be differences?

The reason for three different grades of uncirculated coins is that everything is *not* consistent at the mint. Dies wear down after thousands of strikings, and the impact of the presses can vary slightly. The 1921 peace dollar, for example, required tremendous pressure to achieve a solid strike. Thus, at this writing, the normal strike, which is slightly shallow, costs from $100 to $150 depending upon the dealer. A full strike with everything flawless, and the relief of the design as detailed as possible will cost $500 and up.

Most collectors choose one or the other extremes of condition. They either want the highest-quality, flawless coins known as "gems" or "MS-65-70" to collectors, or they want a well-worn specimen with clear date and design features. Low-budget collectors or collectors trying for completeness of several series of coins, something very expensive to do even with worn coins, will want only well-circulated specimens. Those with higher budgets will stay with uncirculated coins. The grades in between are in limited demand so prices fluctuate very little.

Dealers are rather notorious in the way they describe their coins. "Uncirculated" coins are considered the least expensive of the mint's specimens. They are typical of the thousands of business strikes produced every day by the mint. In the case of the silver dollars, they may even have small marks made when they

Among the increasingly popular U.S. coins are the old commemorative issues that started back in 1893. However, care must be taken to study the quality of the striking. These coins are often rather notoriously poor in condition, and few dealers can supply the entire series in the finest grades.

were tossed into bags in anticipation of being sent to banks for distribution. However, dealers may call them "uncirculated," "brilliant uncirculated", and, occasionally, even "choice uncirculated." A better strike, perhaps made when the die was new, usually is called "choice brilliant uncirculated" and, occasionally, a "gem." Finally, there is the "gem" category, which is a flawless, well-struck coin that has no bag marks (on the silver dollars) and details that make it seem to be the state of the coinmaker's art. One dealer, whom I would never patronize, calls such items "gemmy gems." Honestly!

Notice how the terms seem to mean different things to different dealers? If they are using the same grading guides and are careful about how they study the coins, the coins should look similar when the same descriptive terms are applied. Unfortunately many dealers grade in their own way, relying upon "experience" instead of the standard systems most collectors follow.

What is the answer? You have to find a dealer whose grading and pricing you can trust. This should be done by studying coins from dealer to dealer, comparing his or her grading with the guide books. Then, when you narrow the field a bit, there are some other tests of dealer "quality" you can use.

Is the dealer in good standing with the Better Business Bureau? Call the BBB to ask. The fact that a coin dealer is a *member* of the BBB is a nice "plus" but doesn't mean that the dealer adheres to the code of ethics. The BBB will have files that tell if there have been complaints that were justified and how the complaints were handled.

Is the dealer a member of the Professional Numismatists' Guild? PNG has very strict membership requirements, including the value of the dealer's stock, years in business, and other criteria. There is a code of ethics and an authentification service for determining whether or not an investment coin is genuine. Many good dealers are not members of PNG.

However, a dishonest dealer is not going to stay in PNG very long, and I know at least one dealer who was expelled for improper business and personal actions. If I knew nothing else about a dealer than the fact that he or she was a member of PNG, something the dealer will advertise, I would tend to trust the person.

How long has the dealer been in business in the same community? A dealer who has been in the same location for many years has had to answer to customers who felt they were having problems. A new dealer may eventually become the "established" business you want, several years down the road. But since the new dealer might also fold in six months or a year, I would avoid such persons when buying anything but common coins.

Does the dealer have equipment to allow for at least minimal examination of possibly counterfeit coins? This may mean a microscope of reasonably high power or more sophisticated apparatus. Such equipment is not essential but it will help detect common counterfeits such as a low-value coin that has been made to seem rare by the removal or addition of a mint mark. Any expensive coin should be sent to a professional authentication service such as those mentioned later in this book.

Will the dealer take the time to help educate you about the coins you are buying when he or she is not busy with other customers? If a dealer is interested only in selling coins and not in helping you learn about them, you want to look elsewhere. Perhaps two thirds of the fun in this hobby is learning the background of what you own, not just acquiring the specimens themselves.

If all these criteria are met, you will have a dealer you can trust. Naturally, the recommendations of long-term customers are also pluses, but they may not have the knowledge to accurately judge the person from whom they are buying. The tests I have just mentioned are among the best you can make.

When a coin has any wear at all, it is a circulated coin and will sell for less money than an uncirculated specimen. For many years, collectors frequently kept their coins in cabinets with felt or other fabric lining the drawers. The coins, placed in precut openings, were loose enough so that each time the drawer was pulled out, the coins would slide slightly against the fabric. Over the years, this "cabinet friction" would cause a slight wearing of the coin's surface. Thus you will see advertisements with the designation "uncirculated—cabinet friction" or "BU-Rub" or something similar. These coins are offered at a full uncirculated price but, when you go to sell them, the wear from the drawer will cause the buyer to insist the coin is circulated, a fact that will result in a substantially lower price. Even the dealer from whom you bought the coin is likely to come in with a low bid.

Other dealers call slightly worn coins about uncirculated, borderline uncirculated, uncirculated slider, and similar designations. The fact is that a coin either shows wear or it doesn't. If it shows wear, no matter what the cause, it is a circulated coin and worth less money in the marketplace.

How can you protect your own coins from wear? Never use a coin cabinet or other holder that is loose enough so the coin can slide about. There are custom plastic (Lucite, generally) holders available for specific-size coins and sets of coins, as well as cheaper two-by-two clear holders which can be inserted in albums or special boxes. A cardboard frame surrounds a sandwich of thin plastic, which protects each coin.

Some collectors use "penny boards"—cardboard holders with holes for different dates and mints of various types of cents, nickels, etc., including those of many foreign countries. These are the cheapest holders available. They leave the coins open to air but hold them tightly and keep them from touching one another. Thus they prevent further wear.

Individual two-by-two envelopes, one for each coin, are used by some collectors. Gener-ally they buy an antitarnish tissue and wrap one piece of the special paper around each coin before inserting it into an envelope. These are filed in special containers that fit easily into a safe-deposit box.

When handling coins, always grasp them by the edges so your fingers never touch the front and back surfaces. Wearing cotton gloves can also be a help because it reduces the chance of your getting body oils and finger marks on the coins.

Never clean coins, polish them, or use a brightener to make them appear shinier. It is more than likely that you will create a situation that results in the coins being slightly worn, thus causing a drop of both value and desirability.

Coins that have never been cleaned change color slightly over the years. This toning is desirable to collectors and should not be removed.

In the case of ancient coins, it may be necessary to remove centuries of grime just to see what you have. Hold the coins by their edges in a basin of soapy water. Swirl them around, letting the movement of the water knock the dirt from the surface of the coin. Then rinse each piece, take a clean towel, and lay it on a table. Place the coins on one half the towel, keeping them separated. Then flip the other half of the towel over the coins and let them blot-dry in between. There will be no friction or other abrasion when dried in this manner.

Never stack coins or wrap them with rubber bands. Stacking usually results in scratches. Rubber bands leave marks across the surface of the coins. Some people buy tubes to hold rolls of coins. However, collectors have no interest in owning twenty to fifty of the identical coin, and investors, as the chapter on this subject shows, are being speculative gamblers when they buy rolls rather than single-coin rarities. Thus there is no reason for you to own such tubes.

Every dealer stocks different coins for one reason or another. If the dealer sells only locally, the stock will reflect local interest. Thus, if you are interested in foreign coins, you will find dealers along the northern United States border stocking a wide variety of Canadian coins, and dealers along the nation's southern border stocking Mexican coins. The reason for this is that their customers, living along the borders, have an interest in the country nearest to them. A collector of Mexican coins living in Detroit, for example, may find that he or she has a better selection when buying from a dealer a couple of thousand miles away.

A dealer only stocks what is demanded. However, some dealers advertise in the various hobby publications in order to broaden their market. Since collectors from throughout the country and around the world contact the dealer for coins, the shop can stock a vast array of specimens that might never be sold to a strictly local market.

You should try to find a dealer who has a good supply of the types of coins that most interest you. Not only will you be able to study the coins carefully before you buy them, you will also know that your dealer has contacts in the field and can locate specialized, perhaps rare items for you that are not in stock.

In the smaller communities you may find yourself having to buy coins through the mail when no dealer is close at hand. Major dealers put out periodic catalogs, often heavily illustrated, which are either free or sell for a refundable price of a dollar or two. Smaller dealers advertise their wares extensively on the pages of the hobby publications listed in this book.

Before buying coins through the mail, have as many of the questions about the dealer answered as possible. The same criteria apply when buying through the mail, except for those questions that can only be answered by visiting the shop. The Better Business Bureau of the dealer's city will be quite happy to answer questions about the dealer you make in writing or by long-distance telephone.

If you are going to be buying coins through the mail, it is best to have a post-office box or business address rather than your home address listed. Being known publicly as a coin collector can make you a target for thieves. This is a fact I hate to admit, yet, being realistic, it must be faced. I do not feel the threat is serious enough to warrant your taking up some other hobby, but I do feel that reasonable precautions are in order. These include using a safe-deposit box for rare-coin storage and not giving out your home address when buying coins through the mail or joining an organization such as the ANA.

The problem with having your home address known is that dealers are targets not only of coin thieves but also of thieves seeking files with their customers' addresses. In 1977, for example, a Canadian dealer was robbed of both coins and confidential files he thought were well hidden. The files indicated who his customers were throughout both Canada and the United States. The thieves, who were fortunately caught by police, were going to travel from city to city, burglarizing the people on the list. They had no idea whether the customers bought five dollars in coins a year or five thousand dollars in coins and they didn't care. They felt that the odds for making fairly regular, successful hauls were with them. And their approach was not unique. However, if you don't use your home address, how is someone going to find you readily?

All coins sent through the mail should carry a return privilege stated in writing. Most likely you will be buying the coins through advertisements placed in the various hobby publications devoted to coin collecting. Your rights concerning the return of the coins should be spelled out in the advertisement. Generally, the ads state that you have from seven to ten days to return the coins. However, there can be exceptions.

Some dealers say that you can return any coins for any reason and get a full refund. However, other dealers stress that they must approve your reason for the return. Since many times the reason is a matter of opinion —a disagreement over grading, for example— you can end up on the losing end.

There are also occasional dealers who will not refund your purchase price under any circumstances. Instead they insist upon your taking merchandise of equal value in exchange. This is totally unrealistic for the collector, especially if your interest is in buying a rarity for investment purposes. That dealer may have no other coins in stock that are such good investments. Thus you cannot win with such a dealer.

One example of what can happen with refund requests involved a wealthy collector who bought fourteen thousand dollars in rare coins from a large dealer. He purchased the coins from a catalog that stated, at the beginning, that all returns were subject to the approval of the dealer.

When the coins arrived, the collector was disappointed. He stated that the coins were improperly graded and were worth less money than the dealer charged. Whether this really was the case is not known. It may be that the collector had second thoughts about committing such a vast sum of money to the purchase of the coins and wanted out of the deal. Whatever the reality, he sent them back, asking for a refund.

The dealer returned the coins to the collector along with a letter explaining that the staff had studied the coins in question and found them to be exactly as represented in the catalog. The dealer was sorry that the collector did not agree but the dealer did not feel the reason for the coin return was valid. He would not allow the collector to back out of paying.

The collector was irate, but the dealer was within his rights. The collector went to every hobby organization related to coin collecting, the news media, and anyone else he could get to listen to his story. What the final outcome will be, I do not know. However, it is certain that the dealer acted properly according to the terms stated in writing at the start of the catalog. Thus it is essential that you read such warnings before doing business through the mail. If no return policy is stated, write to the dealer and get a written promise concerning what will happen if you are dissatisfied for any reason.

Another way to purchase coins is through coin auctions. Some dealers privately state that an auction is the best place to sell your coins and the worst place in which to buy them.

The reason for the dealers' cynical comment is that an auction is more than just a place where coins are sold. It is an arena of competition where many people get caught up in a desire to "win." They lose sight of the true value of the object on which they are bidding and concentrate only on the acquisition at any cost. They must emerge triumphant from the competition. They are like gladiators entering an arena to do combat. They take pride in the triumph and forget the cost.

Before attending an auction or sending a bid to one held through the mail, study the coins in which you are interested. Find out how readily available they might be, the normal dealer charge for that same item bought in a coin shop, and the current catalog value. Next consider the fact that dealers normally mark up their prices at least 20 per cent, so you know that a dealer in attendance is liable to bid against you to a level of 80 per cent of expected resale value.

When you begin making bids on relatively common material—coins that can be bought from a number of dealers' shops—limit your bidding to a figure that is 90 per cent to 95 per cent of normal retail. Do not get into competition with some other bidder, each of you topping the other's offer by a few dollars just so one can emerge triumphant. You will only end up paying more than the item is worth. It is better to lose the coins than to overpay.

True rarities are another matter. If a dozen coins exist and one is for sale, you know it may be years before another comes on the market. If you want the coin and can afford it, the ceiling you place on your bidding will be determined only by your personal finances. In fact, usually the highest past auction price for a great rarity becomes the starting bid when the same or a similar specimen comes on the market again.

If you are attending an auction in person, carry with you all the reference material you may need. This means a grading guide book, appropriate catalogs such as the red book, and perhaps a coin newspaper featuring the current prices of the various coins.

Next, study each specimen being offered. If the coins are in a holder, ask to have them removed so the edges can be checked for scratches, gouge marks, and similar problems. Be certain the coin is what you want because, when you are present at the auction, there will be no return privilege. It is assumed that any flaws will be noted in advance and that you will not bid beyond your capacity to pay. There is no valid reason for the return of the coin that you find acceptable before the auction, especially if your only reason is that you got so caught up in the competition that you paid double the true value in order to outbid another collector.

Mail-auction dealers will send catalogs to you for a small fee, generally from three dollars to five dollars, the price covering a copy of the prices realized, which is mailed after the auction is over. These catalogs will be illustrated and the coins described. Since you theoretically have investigated the out-of-town dealer holding the auction in the same manner you would use if you were making a direct-mail purchase, you can probably feel safe with the accuracy of the descriptions. Flaws will be noted, and a coin described as being of high quality should be just that. Thus I would not hesitate to bid by mail.

When you bid through the mail, you cannot tell the company you want five dollars added to the high bid each time someone tops your

offer, as would be the case if you bid in person. What you must do is decide the *maximum* amount of money you will be willing to pay for the coin and use this as your bid.

Mail bidding is handled two ways, again according to the statement made at some point in the catalog you receive. In some cases, your bid is the figure for which you will get the coin, regardless of the lower bid that lost. Thus if you say you will spend twenty-five dollars for a coin and no one bids more than ten dollars, you will get the coin for twenty-five dollars, considerably more than you probably would have paid if you had bid in person.

A second approach, one that is used by a majority of dealers, is to give you the coin for a set dollar amount or percentage over the losing bid. This is usually around five dollars but can be more. Thus, in our previous example of a ten-dollar maximum floor bid compared with your twenty-five-dollar mail bid, the price for which you would get the coin might be just fifteen dollars.

Receipt of the coins is handled in several ways after you make the winning bid. The coin might be mailed to you with the requirement that you pay upon receipt. Or the coin might be held until you send a deposit. There may or may not be a guaranteed return privilege, so be certain you understand all the fine points, in writing, of any particular auction. If the catalog wording is vague, either get a written clarification from the dealer or don't bid.

Occasionally the owner of a great rarity will try to manipulate the price of the coin through an auction. Suppose someone owns a coin for which thirty thousand dollars was paid. A talk with dealers indicates that the probable market value is forty thousand dollars, which is a high figure but not what the owner wants to get. The coin was bought as an investment ten years earlier, and a 33⅓ per cent rise in value over that period is less than could have been earned from bank interest. What does the owner do? He places the coin for auction.

The owner cheats in the auction. He has an

arrangement so the coin has a reserve bid of sixty-five thousand dollars. According to the record, the coin is sold for that high figure. In reality, the buyer is actually the present owner.

Armed with this auction record, which undoubtedly will get played up in the hobby press (names of people making winning bids are never revealed), the owner then arranges for a private sale of the coin. Another hopeful investor spends seventy-five thousand dollars, based on the belief the auction record accurately reflected the market, to buy the coin, and the original owner receives the kind of return he wanted in the first place.

What happens after that? Anything is possible. Sometimes the publicity generates so much interest that the coin continues rising in price, perhaps breaking the one-hundred-thousand-dollar barrier. Other times there is no one else willing to pay even the seventy-five-thousand-dollar figure. When the coin again comes on the market, it might sell for perhaps forty-five thousand dollars, a more realistic value based on demand and rarity. Fortunately this problem is never likely to concern you or me. It is just something of which you should be aware if you are interested in auction purchasing.

There are good and there are bad times to sell your coins, and these are determined by the weather. Coin collecting is most popular during the winter months when people spend more time indoors. When you can't go to the beach, hike in the mountains, or even readily get through the snow to go to a movie, you are likely to want to sit down with your coin collection. You are also likely to go on a buying spree both at your local dealer's shop and through the mail.

During the summer, coin collecting enters a slump period. People go on vacation, play tennis, golf, swim, and engage in all manner of activities outside the home. An occasional rainy day might be devoted to coins but, more likely, it will be spent getting the rod and reel

into shape, cleaning the attic, or practicing putting on the living-room rug. Coins are infrequently enjoyed, and the buying of coins is almost totally stopped.

A renewed flurry of interest occurs briefly during July and August. July is the month the new red book is usually placed on the market, and every collector wants to see whether or not prices have risen enough in the past year so that he or she can retire. In August, the American Numismatic Association traditionally holds its annual convention, during which a major auction takes place. Great rarities come up for sale, and the public becomes aware of the big business that is a part of coin collecting.

What does all this mean to you? Simply that you can save money by buying during the times when people are least interested in their collections. Many dealers, desperate to turn over their stock, reduce prices or offer bargains in special collections. Prices are at their lowest, with no rises contemplated, at least until the new red book comes out. And the competition for coin ownership is so low that auctions offer good buys. If it is possible for you to buy heavily at such times instead of only when you will be spending many hours with your collection in the winter months, you will gain the greatest value from your hobby dollars.

Naturally, the reverse of all this is true when selling your coins. You get the most money when collectors are eager for coins. This means selling during the winter months or consigning your coins to a major auction such as the one held at the ANA convention.

You can also become your own coin dealer when you have coins to sell. For a few dollars, you can advertise in one of the hobby publications, offering your coins for from 5 per cent to 10 per cent less than the retail market. Your overhead is limited to the price of the advertisement, so this figure should give you a substantial profit. However, the one drawback is the potential for customer complaints.

There may be disputes in grading and pricing that you are poorly equipped to handle. Thus, as a beginner, I would sell coins only to dealers even though your return is less.

An alternative to selling your coins through advertisements is to join a coin-collecting club near where you live. You can obtain the names of such organizations from area dealers. These clubs generally have a time set during each meeting when the members can trade, buy, and sell their coins. Excellent deals can be made, providing you keep abreast of the values of your holdings through careful checking of the advertisements in the coin periodicals.

Another way to buy coins is to get them from the country of origin. The United States Mint, for example, has a program in which the public, both here and abroad, can buy proof sets and mint sets (specially packaged, regular-circulation coins in uncirculated condition) for the current year. Similar programs are available abroad.

At times, the foreign mints offer coins directly to collectors. At other times the coins are sold through a dealer who serves as the agent. For example, at this writing, Paramount International, an Ohio dealer, handles the coins from a number of countries, working directly with those governments' mints.

Proof and uncirculated coins sold to collectors by foreign mints should not be looked upon as bargains or potential investment items, though there is always a chance they will become both. The reason is that the prices charged are always fairly high. These special coin sets are high-profit items for the issuing governments, including our own, and there has to be strong collector interest in excess of production to even maintain the issue price. An unpopular set may eventually sell below the issue price, a frequent occurrence with U.S. proof sets of the recent past.

The main reason for buying coins directly from the country of origin is because you enjoy them and know that if you got the same specimens from a dealer, the price would be somewhat higher. Many of these issues are beautiful examples of medallic art and well worth acquiring for that reason alone. However, the chance that these coins will gain in value is slim. Investment should not be a consideration.

Personal checks may be acceptable to some countries, but most want you to use special drafts available through banks. Include airmail postage because surface mail can take six weeks or longer. By writing to the countries, you will be able to obtain full details concerning prices and ordering instructions.

Among the countries offering coins to collectors are:

AFGHANISTAN: Da Afghanistan Bank, Ibn Sina Street, Government Bank, Kabul, Afghanistan

AUSTRALIA: Comptroller of the Mint, Royal Australian Mint, Deakin, A.C.T., Australia 2600

AUSTRIA: Direktion des Osterreichisches Hauptmunzamtes, Postfach 225, A-1031 Wien, Austria

BURUNDI: Banque de la Republique du Burundi, B.P. 705, Bujumbura, Republic of Burundi

CANADA: "Coins Uncirculated," P.O. Box 457, Station A, Ottawa, Ontario K1N 8V5, Canada

CYPRUS: The Central Bank of Cyprus, P.O. Box 1087, Nicosia, Cyprus

DENMARK: Denmark's National Bank, Havnegade 5, 1093 Kobenhaven, K, Denmark

EQUATORIAL AFRICAN STATES: Banque Centrale Libreville, (Boite Postale) B.P. 112, Gabon, Africa; also Banque Centrale Pointe-Noire, (Boite Postale) B.P. 751, Congo, Africa

ETHIOPIA: National Bank of Ethiopia, Manager, Foreign Branch, P.O. Box 5550, Addis Ababa, Ethiopia

FIJI: Central Monetary Authority Numismatic Section, P.O. Box 1220, Suva, Fiji

FOOD AND AGRICULTURE ORGANIZATION OF THE UNITED NATIONS (FAO coins): FAO Coins (Rome), 1776 F Street, N.W., Washington, D.C. 20437

GERMANY (WEST): Verkaufsstelle fur Sammlermunzen der Bundesrepublik Deutschland, Bahnhofstrasse 16–18, D-638 Bad Homburg, West Germany

GHANA: Manager of the Bank of Ghana, P.O. Box 2674, Accra, Ghana

GREAT BRITAIN: The British Royal Mint, 128 Passaic Avenue, Fairfield, New Jersey 07006

GREECE: The Bank of Greece, Treasury Department, P.O. Box 105, Athens, Greece

GUATEMALA: Banco de Guatemala, Apartado Postal 365, Guatemala City, Guatemala

HAITI: Banque Nationale de la République d'Haiti, Head Office, Corner Rue Américaine and Rue Fereu, Port-au-Prince, Haiti

HONDURAS: Banco Central de Honduras, Avenida Juan R. Molina 5A, Calle, Tegucigalpa, Honduras

HUNGARY: Magyar Nemzeti Bank, Szabadsag ter 8, 1850 Budapest V, Hungary

ICELAND: National Bank of Iceland, Reykjavik, Iceland

INDIA: Numismatic Agency of India, 76 South Orange Avenue, South Orange, New Jersey 07079

IRAN: Bank Markazi Iran, Ferdowsi Avenue, P.O. Box 3362, Tehran, Iran

IRAQ: Central Bank of Iraq, Issue Department, P.O. Box 64, Baghdad, Iraq

IRELAND: Central Bank of Ireland, P.O. Box 61, Dublin 2, Ireland

ISRAEL: Israel Government Coins and Medals Corp. Ltd., 5 Ahad Ha'am St., Jerusalem, Israel

ITALY: The Italian Mint, La Zecca, Servizio Numismatico, Via Principe Umberto 4, Rome, Italy

JAPAN: Japan Mint Bureau, Business Section, 1 Shinkawasakicho, Kita-Ku, Osaka, Japan

JERSEY: State Treasury, 31 Broad Street, St. Helier, Jersey, C.I. (U.K.)

JORDAN: Central Bank of Jordan, P.O. Box 37, Amman, Jordan

LEBANON: Banque du Liban, Department du Tresor, B.P. 5544, Beirut, Lebanon

LUXEMBOURG: Caisse D'Epargne de l'État, 1, Place de Metz, Luxembourg, Luxembourg

MACAO: Government Department of Information and Tourism, Macao, China

MALTA, REPUBLIC OF: Malta Coins Distribution Center, Via Bocca di Leone 68, Rome, Italy

MALTA, Sovereign Military Order of Malta: Treasury of the Grand Magistry of Sovereign Military Order of Malta, Via Condotti 64, 00187 Rome, Italy

MOROCCO: Banque du Maroc, Service des Billets et Monnaies, B.P. 445, Rabat, Morocco

NETHERLANDS: Rijks Munt, Leidseweg 90, Postbus 2407, Utrecht, Netherlands

NEW CALEDONIA: Institut d'Émission d'Outre-Mer, B.P. 250, 17 Rue de la République, Nouméa, New Caledonia

NEW ZEALAND: Trae the Treasury, Private Bag, Lambton Quay, Wellington, New Zealand

NIGERIA: Central Bank of Nigeria, Tinubu Square, Lagos, Nigeria

NORWAY: Norges Bank, P.O. Box 735, Oslo 1, Norway

PAKISTAN: Accounts Officer, Master of the Mint, Pakistan Mint, Lahore 9, Pakistan

PHILIPPINES: Central Bank of the Philippines, Cash Department, Roxas Boulevard, Manila, Philippines

PORTUGAL: Casa de Moeda, Avenida Dr. Antonio José de Almeida, Lisbon 1, Portugal

QATAR: Qatar National Bank, P.O. Box 1000, Doha, Qatar

ROMANIA: Cartimex, Calea Victoriei Nr. 126, P.O. Box 134–35, Bucharest, Romania

RWANDA: The Banque National du Rwanda, Kigali, Rwanda

SAN MARINO: General Administrative Secretariat, Republic of San Marino

SINGAPORE: The Singapore Mint, P.O. Box 1334, Republic of Singapore

SOUTH AFRICA: Pretoria Mint, Box 464, Pretoria, South Africa

SPAIN: Fabrica Nacional de Moneda y Timbre, Jorge Juan 106, Madrid 9, Spain

SUDAN: Bank of Sudan, P.O. Box 313, Khartoum, Republic of Sudan

SWITZERLAND: Eidg. Kassen-u. Rechnungswesen, Bundesgasse 3, CH-3003 Bern, Switzerland

SYRIA: Banque Centrale de Syria, Treasury Department, Damascus, Syria

TAIWAN: Business Department of the Bank of Taiwan, Head Office—Business Department, Chungking Road (South), Taipei, Taiwan, China

THAILAND: Royal Thai Mint, 110/7 Pradiphat Road, Saphan Kwai, Bangkok, Thailand

TONGA: Numismatic Section, Treasury, Nukualofa, Tonga

TUNISIA: Banque Centrale de Tunisie, P.O. Box 369, Tunis, Tunisia

TURKEY: Directorate of the Turkish Mint, Darphane Road, Besiktas, Istanbul, Turkey

UNITED STATES: Bureau of the Mint, 55 Mint Street, San Francisco, California 94175

VATICAN CITY: Numismatic Office and Vatican Branch P.O., St. Peter's Square, State of Vatican City

WESTERN SAMOA: Agency of Western Samoa Treasury, 118 King William Street, G.P.O. Box 954, Adelaide, South Australia 5001

YEMEN ARAB REPUBLIC: Official Distribution Center Coins of Yeman, Suite 1006, 575 Madison Avenue, New York, New York 10022

YUGOSLAVIA: Banque Nationale de Yougoslavie, P.O. Box 1010, YU-11001, Belgrade, Yugoslavia

ZAMBIA: Bank of Zambia, P.O. Box 80, Lusaka, Zambia

In addition to the governments listed, four private firms are among the issuing agencies for coins of the world. You should write to them to learn what they currently have available. These include:

FRANKLIN MINT, Franklin Center, Philadelphia, Pennsylvania 19091

ITALCAMBIO, INC., P.O. Box 1358, North Miami, Florida 33161

PARAMOUNT INTERNATIONAL COIN CORPORATION, Paramount Plaza, Englewood, Ohio 45322

SPINK & SON LTD., 5 King Street, St. James's, London S.W.1, England

Regularly updated information on ordering world coins can be found in the *Coin World Almanac* published by Coin World through Amos Press. It is available from most coin dealers.

Among the many coin-collecting publications available are:

COINage, Behn-Miller Publishers, Inc., 16001 Ventura Boulevard, Encino, California 91316

Coin Illustrated, Comstock Publishing Company, Inc., 20121 Ventura Boulevard, Woodland Hills, California 91364

Coins Magazine, Krause Publications, Inc., Iola, Wisconsin 54945. This publishing company also produces *Coin Prices* and the newspapers *Numismatic News* and *World Coin News.*

Coin World, P.O. Box 150, Sidney, Ohio 45367

The Numismatist, American Numismatic Association, P.O. Box 2366, Colorado Springs, Colorado 80901

Collectors seeking access to libraries should consider joining the American Numismatic Association, 818 North Cascade, Colorado Springs, Colorado 80903, as well as the Canadian Numismatic Association. The latter can be joined by writing the General Secretary, P.O. Box 226, Barrie, Ontario, Canada.

There are several authentification services for coins. The best known is the American Numismatic Association Certification Service, 818 North Cascade Avenue, Colorado Springs, Colorado 80903.

Members of the Professional Numismatics Association have their own certification program, which has proven to be excellent. When you deal with a member, who will display the PNG logo, you can request that a rarity be certified before the sale is completed.

Chapter 11

COIN VALUES

Most people who are curious about coins know the excitement of going through their pocket change, an old, long-forgotten piggy bank, or a small box of coins a grandparent kept in the back of a drawer. Some of the coins are so old that you have never seen the designs except in books or coin stores. Other coins are more familiar, yet old enough that you wonder if perhaps they have some value. Since many of these coins may well have greater worth than just the amount stamped on their face, let us explore the potential values of the coins you are most likely to come across.

The values of specific coins mentioned in this chapter will not be given because the coin market has been rising so steadily for so many months that a price stated at the time of writing may be much lower than the value when you read this book. Instead, I will explain some of the better dates to which you should be alert, since they will command a premium if either uncirculated or showing only moderate wear. The annually updated red book, mentioned elsewhere, and the various weekly and monthly publications also cited in this

book will be your best sources for the latest pricing information. This chapter will alert you to the coins to set aside so you do not accidentally spend what might be a precious "nugget" from the potential gold mine in your pocket change.

Regardless of rarity, all silver coins have value beyond their face amount. This means all Franklin half dollars, early Roosevelt dimes, early Washington quarters, and all the silver coins that preceded them. The earliest Kennedy half dollars also have high silver content, as mentioned in another chapter. At this writing, the silver content of the typical silver American coin is worth *approximately* three times face value. Coin dealers vary in what they pay per coin, but many will give you a high trade-in when you use a common silver coin to pay for merchandise. Compare dealer offers within your area, as some will pay a few cents more than others for single pieces and a fairly high premium for large quantities.

Current coinage lacks real market value so long as it is perfectly normal. The only Kennedy half dollar commanding much of a premium is the 1970 half struck by the Denver

Mint (1970-D) because this was not released into circulation. Only specially packaged sets of coins prepared by the mint included this date. However, so many of the special sets were issued that this is not a rarity, and the premium paid for the coin has been constant for quite some time. When the value does not rise steadily, it is an indication that supply equals or exceeds the demand. That is the case with the 1970-D Kennedy half dollar. What little value increase has taken place is probably the result of speculative holdings. The quantity minted is just too large for rarity status.

Even though the 1970-D was only produced in special sets, some people accidentally or deliberately spent the half dollar. Thus these coins have been found in circulation. Although the circulated coins might be considered true rarities, no one cares about that fact. There is no premium paid for the coin just because it has gone into change.

The Eisenhower dollars and the new Susan B. Anthony dollars are also not valuable at this writing or in the foreseeable future. Too many were made for any great value rise to occur among the coins struck for circulation.

It is quite possible that in the relatively near future you will see the prices for Eisenhower dollars rising greatly, and all manner of dealers will be touting the "investment" value of both single coins and rolls of the coins. You will be urged to get in on the ground floor of the next investment wave. The publicity is likely to be intense, and many people will yield to the enticing words being written about the dollars. Don't fall for them!

In the section on investment, the great speculation of the 1960s was mentioned. This is happening again with both the Eisenhower dollars and, to a lesser degree, the Anthony dollars. As soon as the Anthony coin was made official, people began hoarding perfectly common Eisenhower dollars in record numbers. Literally millions of the Eisenhower coins were taken from gambling casinos throughout Nevada by visitors who hoped that their winnings would be increased by the rising value of the coins. There will come a point when the hoarders will take their accumulations of dollars to coin dealers in order to get "rich" by cashing them in. The sudden dumping onto the market of large quantities of the coins will result in a rapid drop in price. Common coins that increased in value artificially will return to either current price levels or a lower figure as everyone gets rid of the coins and the new buyers want fewer specimens than are available on the market. Value, as was mentioned earlier, is dependent upon both supply and demand. The supply is just too great.

The Anthony dollars face the same situation. Release date for the coins was delayed until the mint could saturate the country with them, leaving no chance for high value. However, "investors" put away as many as they could on the assumption that the first year of issue would be the most valuable in the years ahead. This was the case with coins in the past when the first year of issue resulted in only a few thousand coins being placed in circulation, but those days are over. Hundreds of millions of Anthony dollars have been released.

The exception to the common date syndrome occurs when the mint makes a mistake. The collecting of mint errors is a growing hobby, and all mint mistakes increase the value of coins, though sometimes only by a few cents.

For example, suppose you opened a roll of half dollars and, in the middle of them, was a clad coin that had somehow missed the press. There is no design on the front or back, yet the blank or "planchet," as it is called, managed to leave the mint. Such an item would be worth several dollars.

Another common mistake is a clipped planchet. The coin is struck with the design but part of the planchet was accidentally cut off at the mint before the striking. Again a premium is paid.

Sometimes a blank planchet for one coin gets struck on the wrong press with the wrong dies. Thus you might find a quarter planchet with a half-dollar design. The design will be incomplete, of course, since the half-dollar design is meant to cover a larger surface area.

There are numerous other mint mistakes. A filled die might result in one digit of a date being missing or perhaps the coin has the motto "In God Trust" with the word "We" missing. Any number of problems can occur, and the alert student of pocket change can make a profit from even the most seemingly common of coins. After all, only a tiny fraction of the coins, sometimes as few as one or two in a run, ever are mistakes. The mint's quality controls are just too good to allow great quantities of slipups to escape detectors. However, they do occur, and the alert collector looking closely at pocket change is likely to find one or more that can be saved or sold for a premium even when the date is normally a common one.

The Franklin half dollars are coins that turn up with relative frequency, especially when someone has an old piggy bank. However, the total number of these halves has steadily declined overall. This is because these coins were melted in fairly large numbers after such melting became legal. As a result, a number of formerly common dates are now scarce, though the value of these coins will be determined by the amount of wear they have seen.

The highest-priced coin among the Franklin halves is the 1949-S. All the 1949 half dollars are fairly scarce, but those struck by the San Francisco Mint command the highest premium in all conditions. If you find any with this date, though, you would do well to save them.

The first year for Franklin half dollars, 1948, is also a year that finds higher-value coins. Other key dates for which to watch are the halves struck by the Denver Mint in 1950 and 1951. Coins struck by other mints in those years are also of interest, but their

values are less. In fact, you will do well with almost any of the 1948 through 1953 coins, all years in which mintages were relatively low. None of these coins are rarities but they have all been rising steadily in value and are frequently found in circulation.

The other coin for which to watch is the 1955. Look closely at coins bearing this date. On some you will notice a mint error called a die break. It has left a line on Franklin's teeth that makes him look like he has fangs. Is it any wonder that the coin bears the nickname "Bugs Bunny" half?

The Washington quarter dates to watch are fairly numerous, though the condition determines their value. A number of the years saw almost every coin go into circulation, with just a handful retained uncirculated. This means that the uncirculated specimen is extremely costly, while coins showing even slight wear will be worth just three dollars or four dollars. Among such coins are the 1943 quarters struck at the San Francisco and Denver mints, the 1942 San Francisco strike, the Denver Mint coins for 1939, 1940, 1941 and, to a lesser degree, 1942.

The 1932 Washington quarter struck by Philadelphia (no mint mark) is only expensive when uncirculated. However, even a well-worn 1932 struck by Denver or San Francisco will command a high premium.

Additional quarters to save include the 1934-D, the 1935-D, 1935-S, 1936-D, 1936-S, 1937-D, 1937-S, 1938-D, 1938-S, and the 1940-D. Uncirculated or barely worn coins dated before 1945 all command reasonably high premiums.

Remember that finding early quarters with little wear is not that unusual. Many people saved the coins for one reason or another over the years, forgetting about them until much later. When your parents or grandparents move from a house to an apartment, when you finally get around to cleaning that attic or really seeing what's in the drawers of those chests you haven't used for years, you are likely to find these old hoards. Their face value may only be four dollars or five dollars, but the dates and mint marks could reveal an actual worth of many times that much.

None of the Roosevelt dimes have any real numismatic value, though the coins dated 1949 and 1949-S are worth several dollars in better conditions. Since no one knows just how many of the early silver dimes of this type have been melted for their bullion, some of the earlier dates may increase in value as evidence of scarcity appears. If you want to save the dates with the greatest potential, set aside all you find dated 1949, regardless of the mint mark, the 1950-S, and the 1951-S.

The Jefferson nickels have a number of dates that command premiums and that are still being found in change. The 1950-D, for example, is worth several dollars even when circulated. It is not an expensive coin at best but it does command a premium and it is found in pocket change. Other dates to watch include the 1939-D, 1939-S, and the silver issues struck during the war years, as mentioned earlier.

Lincoln cents offer a wide range of dates commanding premiums, as well as mint errors. Among the most valuable are the ones dated 1909-S and showing the designer's initials— V.D.B. Collectors refer to this coin as the 1909-S V.D.B. to distinguish it from the less rare but also valuable 1909-S, which did not have the designer's initials.

The 1914-D and 1931-S are also good dates. Less valuable but worth seeking are the 1910-S, 1911-D and 1911-S, 1912-S and 1912-D, 1913-S, 1914-S, 1915-S, 1922-D, 1924-D, 1926-S, and 1931-D.

In 1922, a die problem resulted in a mint error at the Denver Mint. Only the Denver Mint struck Lincoln cents that year, a fact that means that all 1922-dated Lincoln cents should have the "D" mint mark. However, the problem die resulted in the "D" being only partially struck on some coins and not struck at all on others. As a result, the 1922 with no

mint mark showing is extremely prized by collectors.

In 1955 and again in 1972, a quantity of Lincoln cents were struck twice instead of once. The image of Lincoln, the date, and all the lettering are doubled. Looking at the coin is a little like a nearsighted person trying to read small numbers without the aid of eyeglasses. Everything looks slightly blurred, though the two impressions actually are distinct. When you find such coins, you can be certain of a high resale price.

Walking-Liberty half dollars preceded the Franklin halves, and these coins are all worth saving. Interest is strong in this magnificent design, and while some dates may only be worth three or four dollars, that price reflects what has been a regular rise in value in recent months.

The greatest rarities in terms of well-circulated coins include all the 1921-dated specimens, the coins struck by the three mints in 1916, and the 1938-D. A rather odd situation occurred in 1917 that confuses some collectors. Coins struck by the Denver and San Francisco mints do not have the mint marks in the same location. The letters "D" or "S" may be found on either the obverse or the reverse of these coins. You need to check both sides. Another odd fact: When a 1917 coin struck by the Denver Mint is slightly worn, the coins with the mint mark on the obverse command more money than those with the mint mark on the reverse. However, when the coins are uncirculated, you will be ahead with the "D" on the reverse.

Standing-Liberty quarters are also good items to save, regardless of date, though you will find that many have the dates worn away. The dates were raised just enough above the surface of the coins so that an erosion of the metal resulted in coins whose design is clear but the year when struck cannot be determined.

The rarest date Standing-Liberty quarters are the 1916 and what is known as the

1918/17-S. This latter coin is not a mint error but what is known as an overdate. This happens in numerous series of coins and is the result of the mint using an old die after the year changes. In this case, the San Francisco Mint started 1918 with a die dated 1917. The die was probably unused but, by law, the new coins had to be struck with the new date. Rather than throw away an otherwise usable die, the engraver stamped the "18" over the "17." Since relatively few coins were struck from that die, the overdates are rare.

The best way to spot an overdate is with a fairly strong magnifying glass. If you look within the loops of the "8," you will see the bold line of the "7." It is stronger on some coins than others but you will not have trouble spotting it.

A third date that is extremely valuable, though only when uncirculated or when it has seen limited wear, is the 1927-S. Well-circulated examples command a premium, but nowhere near the figure of the higher grades.

The Mercury dime series has two overdates of its own. In 1942, both the Philadelphia and Denver mints had 1941-dated dies they restamped. The "1" is quite obvious with this overdate since it seems to close the loop of the "2." These coins are technically known as the 1942/1 and the 1942/1-D. These coins have been found in circulation over the years and conceivably are still lurking in old jars filled with small change.

There are three other Mercury dime dates that are quite scarce even when well circulated. These are the coins from the Philadelphia and Denver mints dated 1921, as well as the 1916-D. Other good dates you might find include the 1917-D, 1918 from all three mints, 1919-D, 1919-S, 1925-D, 1926-S, 1927-D, 1928-D, and 1931-D. Most of the Mercury dimes command a premium when uncirculated, though the dates not specifically mentioned in this chapter drop in price rather quickly as they show increasing signs of wear.

The buffalo nickel series is unusual in that it has both two overdates and a mint error, all of which you might find in circulation. One overdate was typical of others just described. This is the 1918/17-D. The other overdate, a more common one, occurred in 1938. This time the marked year was not changed but the coin went from mint to mint. It was originally a die for the San Francisco Mint and had been engraved with the "S." Then the die was used in Denver and a new mint mark appeared over the old. Thus the coin has the lines of the "S" visible inside the opening of the "D." The coin is known as the 1938-D/S variety.

The earliest coins of the twentieth century include the Indian-head cents. All Indian-head cents are climbing steadily in value, and it would be a good idea to set them aside regardless of wear. A few years ago, Indian-head cents that were well worn and extremely common sold for fifteen cents each. Today they sell for from seventy cents to eighty-five cents each on the retail market. They are obviously not valuable, but interest is rising and the prices are going with them.

Among the best Indian-head-cent dates are the 1908-S and the 1909-S. These are the only Indian-head cents struck by the San Francisco Mint. All the rest were struck in Philadelphia. The 1894 cent is also a good one, though nowhere near as valuable. All cents struck before the early 1880s are of value, with some, such as the 1877, worth a couple of hundred dollars even when well worn. However, these earliest of dates appear rarely.

The Liberty-head nickel was introduced in 1883 and the coins minted after 1900 are frequently found among old hoards and, occasionally, even in change. Among the twentieth-century specimens, only the 1912-S and 1912-D are of real value when circulated. However, all the dates showing just slight wear, as well as the nickels struck before 1897, are worth saving and one, the 1885, is valuable in all grades.

The Barber dimes were introduced in 1892 and still appear in old hoards. All are of value in the higher grades, and the coins have shown moderate price rises even when common and well worn. One reason for the common-date price rise is the silver content, and a second reason is increased collector interest. I would set them all side but, of the ones struck after 1900, be alert to the 1901-S, 1903-D, and 1904-S. These three command an extremely high premium in all grades as, to a lesser degree, does the 1913-S.

Barber quarters are like Barber dimes in that they are all worth setting aside. However, the true rarities struck after 1900 include the 1901-S and the 1913-S. The 1909-O is fairly common but still commands a much higher-than-average premium in all conditions.

Barber half dollars fit the same pattern as the other Barber-design coins. Of those struck after 1900, keep alert for the 1901-S, 1904-S, 1905-O, 1913, 1914, and 1915-dated issues.

Silver dollars are of two varieties—peace and Morgan designs. Both were struck in large quantities and frequently saved. Sometimes they were saved by parents and grandparents who liked to have them on hand for gifts to children, grandchildren, nieces, and nephews. At other times they were set aside by the people who received them as gifts, then forgotten as the years passed. Still others were deliberately put away in the 1960s when it was learned that they would be withdrawn from circulation. Whatever the reason they were set aside, though, you are likely to come across one or more of these coins. All of them are worth retaining if only because of their intrinsic worth and the fact that an increasing number of people are collecting silver dollars today.

Of the silver dollars you are likely to find in circulation, the dates to note include the peace type 1921, 1927, 1927-D, 1927-S, 1928, 1934, and 1934-S. The Morgan dollar design was also struck in 1921 but in such large quantity that they do not have much of a premium except when uncirculated. Other good dates after 1900 include the 1900-S, 1901, 1901-S, 1902-S, 1903-S, 1903-O, and 1904-S. A large quantity of pre-1900 silver dollars in the Morgan design series are also excellent. Among the valuable are the 1879-CC, 1880-CC, 1881-CC, 1885-CC, 1888-S, 1889-CC, 1892-CC, 1893, 1893-CC, 1893-O, 1893-S, 1894, 1895-O, 1895-S, and 1899.

Circulation finds are no longer what they were before silver coins began disappearing from circulation. You are less likely to find pre-1964 dimes, quarters, and half dollars in your change, but that does not mean that they don't continue to pass from hand to hand during the course of a business day, waiting for an alert collector to spot them. These are also the coins that you *are* likely to find in old savings banks, tossed casually into a drawer, or otherwise hidden away. By following the guidelines in this chapter, you may discover a gold mine disguised as a piggy bank long forgotten on a closet shelf.

Chapter 12

COIN DICTIONARY

There are a number of terms relating to coins and money that you are liable to encounter when talking with dealers and collectors or while reading other books. To help you understand the most common ones, the following brief dictionary has been prepared.

ACCUMULATION: This is a grouping of coins that remain unidentified, unsorted, and otherwise unstudied. It is not a collection but may result from someone tossing pocket change into a container each day, then passing the filled container to a family member interested in coins.

ADJUSTMENT: When a planchet (coin blank) used in the coinmaking process weighs more than the law allows, it is filed before striking the coin. This occurred frequently in the eighteenth century, and the marks sometimes remained after the coining process, resulting in the notation "adjustment marks" in a dealer's descriptions of such coins.

AEGINA: This is the Greek island where the earliest coins were struck in the seventh century B.C. The coins bore the turtle, symbol of Aphrodite (also known as Astarte). Coins

had earlier been made in Lydia, but these were little more than marked lumps of silver. It was natural for coins as we know them today to evolve in Aegina, as it was a major trade center.

AES: A Latin word meaning both copper and bronze.

AES GRAVE: A one-pound weight of copper or bronze used as money.

AES RUDE: Unmarked, rough bronze pieces used as weights rather than coins as we know them.

AES SIGNATUM: These were bronze bars, ingots, and similar objects stamped with a symbol or depiction of an animal. They are occasionally sold during an ancient-coin auction, but no one knows for certain whether they were used as money.

ALLOY: The mixing of more than one metal to produce a stronger, less-valuable, or otherwise altered coin.

ALTERED: A deliberately changed coin, often for dishonest reasons. The 1916 Mercury-head dime is a relatively common coin uncirculated. The 1916-D (struck by the Denver Mint rather than the Philadelphia Mint) is extremely valuable. Some dishonest individuals cut a D mint mark from a common-date Mercury dime, then carefully alter a 1916 so that it appears to have the 1916-D date. Actually the D is just cemented to the metal.

ANGEL: This was a gold coin, first called an angel-noble, that was introduced by England's Edward IV in 1465. The earliest coins show St. Michael defeating Satan on one side and a ship bearing a shield on the other. The coins were used during the royal-touch ceremony where Kings would "cure" people of scrofula through the divine magic of their touch—or so they believed.

ANNA: A copper coin of India valued at one-sixteenth rupee (a fraction of a U.S. cent).

ASSAY: A test of a coin to determine the weight, fineness, and consistency of its metal. An assay piece is a coin that has been set aside for this type of testing.

AUREUS: This was the standard gold coin of ancient Rome. It was the equivalent of twenty-five denarii or one hundred sestertii in the Roman system. It was created by Julius Caesar, who first put it into circulation in approximately 49 B.C.

AX MONEY: The name for a type of copper currency used by the Indian natives of Mexico during the pre-Columbian period.

BAG MARKS: Abrasive marks found on otherwise uncirculated coins, most commonly silver dollars. These marks were made when the coins were tossed into bags before shipment to banks.

BARONIAL COINS: During the Middle Ages, coinage in Germany, France, and Italy was often handled by numerous dukes, lords, barons, and other of noble birth. In other countries, the right to mint coins was reserved solely for the central government.

BARTER: The exchange of goods and services according to a value system agreed upon by the parties doing the trading. It was the system used prior to the invention of coins.

BILLION: An alloy of copper and silver with the copper being the dominant metal.

BINGLE: This is the term used for a token— an unauthorized coinlike object used for trade and often issued by merchants. Originally the term referred only to the tokens used during the 1935 colonization of the Matanuska Valley region of Alaska.

BIT: One eighth of a Spanish dollar. Also known as a real. Two bits equaled twenty-five cents.

BOX COINS: These are coins literally made into boxes. The obverse and reverse sides of two similar coins are joined together after hollowing out the centers. They are threaded for screwing together. Often they were filled with a variety of miniature items. They were most popular during the sixteenth century in the German states.

BRACTEATE: This is a thin silver- or gold-leaf coin that was popular during the twelfth and thirteenth centuries in central Europe.

BRASS: An alloy of approximately 90 per cent copper and the rest another metal, usually tin.

CABINET FRICTION: The surface wear, usually of one side only, experienced by a coin kept in a cabinet. Each time the drawer is pulled out, the coin slides slightly in its trough. The wear is not from circulation but the coin is devalued by collectors all the same.

CARTWHEEL: Originally a massive two-penny piece made from copper and issued by George III. It was struck in 1797 by Matthew Boulton at the Soho Mint in Birmingham, England. The term has since been used to describe large coins such as silver dollars.

CASH: A Chinese coin made from copper alloy. A large hole is in the middle so numerous coins can be strung together, usually in lengths of fifty to one hundred coins each.

CAST COINS: These were coins made by taking a clay or, occasionally, wooden mold, then pouring molten metal into it. It is also a cheap, fairly rapid method of making forgeries.

CHOP MARKS: These were punched impressions applied by Chinese and Indian banks or other financial offices. They attested that the weight and metal content of the coin so punched was proper. Chop marks are common on coins such as the U.S. trade dollar, which were used for overseas business payments.

CLASHED DIES: When an obverse and a reverse die come together without a planchet or coin blank in place, they will damage each other. These clash marks effect the coinmaking process. Coins made from that pair of clashed dies will show traces of the mirror image of the dies on the opposite side of the coin.

CLIPPING: When coins were hammered during the early days of coinage, some people would clip a metal rim around the coins. The coins appeared undamaged to the casual observer while the person doing the clipping had enough extra metal to make a small profit when it was melted with other clippings, then sold.

COB MONEY: These were crude silver coins produced in the Spanish colonies. They were cut from silver bars and had highly irregular borders.

COIN: A piece of metal that has been marked in some manner to show it is of a set weight and fineness. It is issued under the authorization of some government.

COMMUNION TOKEN: The communion token is a church token whose history dates back to the Scottish Presbyterian Church. The token, made from lead or pewter primarily, was issued the day before a communion service to those intending to take communion. The

first ones were used as early as 1635 and were meant to prevent government spies from entering the church during the ceremony. The tokens were generally square and the first ones bore the initial of the parish. Later tokens were embellished with the date and the minister's initials.

CONSECRATION COIN: When a Roman Emperor or member of his family was elevated to the rank of a god, a coin was struck in honor of the event. The coin would have the word "DIVUS" for a man and "DIVA" for a woman. Many of the coins have renderings of the event, usually showing the honored person's funeral pyre.

CONSULAR COINS: These are Roman Republic coins that do not have the family name of the issuer. They were struck by order of the consuls, according to one theory, which is how they once were believed to have gotten their name. However, it is now known that this was not necessarily the case.

COUNTER: This is a small disc, usually made from brass, that was placed on a checkered cloth and used to keep track of business accounts. They were shaped like a coin, and the name has now become synonymous with many imitation coins. During the Victorian era, brass counters were turned out in large number and often were mistaken for ancient coins.

CROWN: This is the general term for large silver coins about the size of the American silver dollar. The actual size is usually from thirty-three to forty-two millimeters in diameter. Anything larger is called a multiple crown.

DALER: A Swedish word for dollar. In 1644, Sweden struck a special ten-daler coin that weighed just under twenty pounds.

DEBASEMENT: The altering of a coin to reduce its intrinsic worth. Some ancient coins were issued in brass with a thin silver wash, then passed as though they were true silver coins.

DIE: This is a piece of hard metal that has been engraved with either the obverse or the reverse of a coin or a metal. The design is prepared in a form known as intaglio, which means that when it is struck against the metal planchet, the design will be stamped on the coin in a raised manner.

DINAR: An Arabian gold coin that originated in A.D. 696.

DIRHEM: An Arabian silver coin very similar to the gold dinar.

DOUBLOON: A large gold coin struck by Spain and the Spanish mints in the New World. It made its appearance during the fourteenth century.

DRACHMA: This was the standard for silver coinage in ancient Greece. It was originally a measure of weight.

DUCAT: This was usually a gold coin, though occasionally they were silver, which was issued in various parts of Europe starting in the middle of the twelfth century. The first issue, minted by Roger II of Sicily for the Duchy of Apulia, bore the motto *Sit tibi, Christe, datus, Quem Tu regis, iste Ducatus*, which meant "Unto Thee, O Christ, be dedicated this Duchy that Thou rulest." It was from the word *Ducatus* that this coin and others like it received the name ducat.

ELECTRUM: A metal used by the ancient Greeks for some of their coinage. It was a natural blend of approximately three parts gold and one part silver, copper, and/or other metal. It usually was amber-colored.

ELONGATED COIN: This is an oval "coin" or medalet. Usually a cent was placed under a roller to elongate it. Often one side was scraped to the copper, then an inscription added.

ENCASED POSTAGE STAMP: A metal, plastic, or other holder into which a postage stamp was placed, then covered with thin mica or other material. The device was used as a coin in areas where there was a coin shortage.

ESCUDO: This is the standard Spanish crown and was struck in both gold and silver. It was equal in value to the French *écu* and the Italian *scudo*.

ESSAY: This is a trial coin rather than a regular issue.

EXONUMIA: These are numismatic items that are not prepared by a government body. They include tokens, especially those made by merchants, medals, scrip, and similar items. Someone who studies this field is known as an exonumist.

FARTHING: This is a British coin that was once the literal quarter of a silver penny. The penny would be cut into either halves (a halfpenny) or quarters, the farthing. Later coins of this value were specifically struck. The first copper farthing was struck in 1672. The last farthings were struck in 1956.

FEUCHTWANGER METAL: Dr. Lewis Feuchtwanger developed a copper-nickel alloy he wanted used for American coinage. It contained 53 per cent copper, 29 per cent zinc, and 18 per cent nickel. Cents and three-cent pieces were struck as a trial back in 1837. These were tokens rather than coins and are fairly numerous.

FIDDLER'S MONEY: These were small silver coins given to fiddlers playing at wakes and festivals in England.

FLAN: A blank piece of metal cut in the shape of a coin. It is struck to produce a coin or a medal.

FLEUR DE COIN (Abbreviated FDC): This is a French term that describes a freshly minted coin. In the United States, the word uncirculated is used.

FLORIN: A gold coin of the last half of the thirteenth century. It was struck in Florence, Italy, and bore the figure of St. John the Baptist on the obverse and a lily on the reverse. The lily was a flower used to symbolize the city of Florence, and the coin was known as the *fiorino d'oro,* Italian for "little gold flower." The name was shortened to florin.

FUGIO CENT: This was a coin authorized by the Continental Congress in 1787. It was thus the first American coin.

GAZZETTA: A small, sixteenth-century copper coin struck by Venice.

GHOST PENNY: George V (1911–27) struck English pennies that were so poor that the image of one side often showed through to the other. This was termed ghosting because of the faint extra image.

GROAT: In the Middle Ages, this term was applied to all thick silver coins.

GUINEA: A British gold coin struck originally from gold found in the Guinea Coast of West Africa.

GUN MONEY: James II issued this Irish emergency money in 1689 and 1690. It was made from scrap metal that included old cannons along with such items as kitchen utensils.

HACIENDA TOKEN: This was a token used in Latin America to pay laborers. The tokens were issued by land owners who also owned the places where they could be redeemed. This bound the laborer to the land owner instead of giving him freedom to spend the tokens where he so chose.

HAMMERED COINS: This was a process of coinmaking used until 1662 by most countries. A rough coin blank was made, placed between two dies, then held with a pair of tongs. Then the unit was hit with a heavy mallet, leaving an impression on the blank.

HARD-TIMES TOKENS: From 1832 to 1844, numerous political tokens were issued in the United States. These copper tokens were meant to ease a severe shortage of cents but were made by private individuals rather than the government. Many of the designs attack President Andrew Jackson.

HOG (HOGGE) MONEY: These were copper coins of the Bermuda Islands where ship's captain Sir George Somers was forced ashore in 1609. The islands were inhabited by vast quantities of pigs and the coins show the hogs as a design element.

INCUSE: This is a term applied to a coin design that is sunk into the flan or planchet. Only one coin, a five-dollar Indian-head gold piece designed by Bela Pratt, was issued with incuse design by the United States Mint. All other coins have a raised design.

INGOT: This term means any piece of metal made from a mold, though the original term referred to the mold itself.

INTRINSIC VALUE: The worth of the metal from which a coin is made rather than the face value. A U.S. gold twenty-dollar coin today has an intrinsic worth many times its face value.

JETON: A form of counter as well as a game piece.

JOHANNES: A gold coin of Portugal that first appeared during the eighteenth century.

JUGATE: Two or more heads either overlapping or joined together.

KNIFE MONEY: Knife money was introduced in China during the seventh century B.C. It was a miniature of the tool and equaled the value of that tool. In Africa, actual knives have been valued as money.

LEATHER MONEY: This is reference to dried skins that were used as barter objects by the ancients. Leather tokens have also been issued as necessity money during wartime in many European countries.

LEGAL TENDER: This is money that may be given to pay debts and cannot be refused by creditors under strict legal conditions.

LEPTON: A term used by the ancient Greeks to describe any small copper coin.

LOVE TOKEN: This was a coin, often bent to insure special, almost magical properties, that was given as a token of affection. Some have the coin design rubbed off, then elaborately re-engrave the piece with hearts, flowers, and similar designs.

MAUNDY MONEY: This is a set of four small silver coins including a penny, twopence, threepence, and fourpence. They were first struck by Charles II for distribution to the poor on Maundy Thursday. The sets of coins were given to an equal number of men and women; the total of each sex equaled the monarch's age.

MEDAL: A piece of metal, often shaped like a coin, meant to honor an event, person, or place. It is not meant to be used for payment of debts and is not legal tender.

MILLED MONEY: This is a reference to coins produced through the use of a screw press, the power for which was supplied by either horse or water mills.

MINT MARK: A symbol, usually a letter, that designates the mint where coins were struck. In the United States, only the Philadelphia Mint fails to put a mint mark on the coins it strikes (with the exception of the silver five-cent pieces used during World War II; the ones from Philadelphia bear a "P" mint mark). The other mints use the letters "D" (Dahlonega, Georgia, Mint from 1838 to 1861 and Denver, Colorado, from 1906 to date); "C" (Charlotte, North Carolina); "O" (New Orleans, Louisiana); "S" (San Francisco, California); and "CC" (Carson City, Nevada).

MITE: Any small coin of little worth. The Bible speaks of the widow's mite in Mark 12:42, where it says: "And there came a certain poor widow, and she threw in two mites, which make a farthing." Scholars believe the widow's mites were actually two perutas, the smallest Jewish coins struck at the time.

MULE: Any coin, medal, or token having an obverse design that does not match the reverse design that is supposed to be part of the regular production issues.

NECESSITY MONEY: An unusual type of money made when regular coinage is impossible. Originally this was the money made from cardboard, dried skins, and anything else available when a city was under siege. Later it refererred to tokens used during coin shortages and similar periods when regular issues were not obtainable.

NOBLE: The noble was a gold coin first struck in 1344 by Edward III. The name means "excellent" coin and was probably chosen as a way of describing the quality of the gold it contained.

NORTHWEST TOKENS: These 1820 dated tokens were used by fur traders in Western Canada, Washington State, and Oregon. They were valued at one beaver—actually one beaver skin, an item that had long been a barter object.

NUMISMATICS: This refers to the study, science, and/or collecting of coins, medals, paper money, and similar items. The person who engages in such activities is known as a numismatist.

OBOL: A small silver coin of ancient Greece. It was valued at one-sixth drachma.

OBVERSE: The side of the coin that has the more important design. Usually this meant the side showing the face of a god or a ruler. This side is frequently called "heads."

OVERDATE: When a coinage year ended, the mint occasionally had dies left over with the previous year's date on them. The engraver would take a new last digit and punch it over the old. Usually the old digit is visible to some degree under the new number and the overdate becomes obvious. In the Mercury-dime series, for example, there is an overdate struck in 1942. Collectors refer to this as "1942/1" or "1942 over 1."

OVERSTRIKE: This occurs when an entirely new coin design is struck on an existing coin rather than a blank planchet. This frequently occurred in areas under siege. Old coins from other areas that were scrounged in the town would be overstruck with a design and denomination that would be acceptable on a local basis.

PAPAL COINAGE: In the years 772–95, Pope Adrian I initialed the striking of an ecclesiastical coinage for the Papal States. He struck deniers that were similar in design to the Byzantine coins. When the Church was at its strongest in the twelfth century, the silver coins were stamped with the legend ROMA CAPUT MUNDI, which translated to "Rome the head of the world." The series of coins ended when the Papal States became a part of Italy in 1871. In 1929, with the Vatican again independent as a city-state, the Popes resumed the issuing of coins.

PATTERN: This is a proposed coin that may have a different design, date, or metal content than the regular issue. Often a pattern coin will never be seen in circulation because the design was rejected. At other times the pattern design becomes a regular issue. In 1883, for example, the United States introduced the Liberty-head nickel. Prior to that, a shield design dominated the nickel coinage. However, when a change was contemplated the year before, a pattern with the new Liberty-head design was struck. Thus there are a small number of pattern Liberty-head nickels dated 1882 in the hands of collectors. Pattern coins are never released into general circulation, however, and U.S. patterns struck after 1916 are not legal to own. In some countries the words "Essai" or "Prova" denote a pattern.

PESO: This is the Spanish milled dollar or eight-reales coin. It was usually a silver coin of one ounce in weight. It is also called a piastre.

PETITION CROWN: This was an unusual coin struck by Thomas Simon, a mint engraver in England who had lost favor with the King. In 1663 he struck a pattern crown meant to convince King Charles II that he was skilled enough to handle the designing of coins that the King wanted to farm out to a foreign engraver. Around the edge of the petition crown are the words: "Thomas Simon most humbly prays your Majesty to compare this his tryall piece with the Dutch and if more truly drawn & emboss'd more gracefully order'd and more accurately engraven to relieve him." The King preferred the foreign concept, however, and no more than twenty of the special crowns are known.

PIASTRE: The standard coin unit for Turkey and other Mediterranean countries. The Turkish pound was equal to 100 piastres.

PICKER'S CHIT: This is another type of token given to laborers. In this case, it was issued for a set amount of produce that was picked and could be redeemed in either money or merchandise.

PLANCHET: A flat blank piece of metal which is stamped into a coin.

PLATE MONEY: These were giant pieces of copper cut into squares and weighing as much as six pounds each. They were used in Sweden during the last half of the seventeenth century and the first half of the eighteenth century at a time when silver was hard to find.

PLUGGED MONEY: These were tin farthings and halfpennies struck by Charles II and James II of England. A small plug of copper was inserted into the coins to prevent counterfeiting.

PROOF: This is a coin made from polished dies and a polished blank. The sharpness and detail are flawless and the coin has a mirrorlike effect. Around the start of the twentieth century there were matte proofs made that have a finely granulated surface appearance. These are all specially struck and sold at a premium.

PROOFLIKE: This is an uncirculated coin which has been specially handled to insure a mirror surface. It is not the flawless strike of an actual proof but does experience more care and special handling during preparation than the regular-issue coins.

PUFFIN: Puffin and half-puffin coins were illegal bronze coins struck by M. C. Harman, a

British subject who lived on Lundy Island in the British Channel. Harman declared himself a King in 1929 and had the coins made. The British Government, not recognizing Harman's "royalty," declared the coins to be illegal.

REAL: This is a small Spanish coin equal to one-eighth real and also known as a "bit."

REDDITE CROWN: This is another coin of Thomas Simon. Unlike the petition crown, this coin has no special message to the King. Instead it reads *Reddite Quae Caesaris Caesari* or "Render unto Caesar the things that are Caesar's."

RESTRIKE: Any coin or medal reproduced from the original dies but at a date later than when the originals were struck. The restrike is usually meant for sale to collectors rather than for circulation.

REVERSE: The side of the coin with the less important design. This is frequently called the "tails" side because, on American coins, the rendering of the eagle is found on the reverse. Ancient Roman coins showing two different leaders will have the more important person's face on the obverse, the less important individual's face on the reverse. When two faces appear on the obverse, this tells the people that the leaders are sharing power equally.

SACRAMENTAL TOKENS: These are tokens with religious significance such as the communion tokens.

SCUDO: This is the Italian silver crown used first in the late sixteenth century. It was sometimes struck in gold as well.

SEIGNORAGE: This was a charge placed against bullion that was turned into coins. When someone brought bullion to the mint, this charge was extracted before the coins were returned.

SHEKEL: This was originally a Babylonian unit of weight. Later it became the principal silver coin of the Hebrews. As such it made its first appearance around the time Nero ruled the Roman Empire.

SHOOTING FESTIVAL COINS: These were Swiss five-franc pieces prepared to serve as prizes during shooting contests, but they also circulated to some degree. They were legal tender.

SIEGE PIECE: These were makeshift coins known as necessity money. They were produced when a city was under siege and did not have access to normal metal supplies and/or coin-making equipment. For additional information, see the listing for "gun money."

SILLY HEAD: A derogatory description of certain coin designs. It was probably first used to describe the Irish halfpenny of 1766 on which George III appeared. Later it was applied to the U.S. large cent of 1839. There was also a U.S. large-cent design called a "booby head."

SKILLING: This is a tiny copper coin worth approximately one-quarter cent. It was used in northern Germany and Scandinavia.

SLUG: The most common use for this word is in reference to a blank or token meant to operate a coin-operated machine. However, it also refers to the fifty-dollar gold pieces produced in California before the establishment of the San Francisco Mint.

SOLIDUE (SOLIDI): The Roman emperor Constantine struck this thick gold coin from approximately A.D. 312. For many years it was the standard gold coin of Europe.

SOU: The common name for the French five-centime piece and halfpenny.

SOU TOKENS: These were copper tokens issued by the Bank of Montreal during the period when Canada had a shortage of coins.

SOVEREIGN: This was originally a large English gold coin that took its name from the portrait of the ruler shown on the obverse. The coin was first struck by King Henry VII in 1489. The sovereign became a much smaller coin under George III. In 1817, King

George III issued the small sovereigns with the image of St. George slaying the dragon.

SPADE MONEY: This was an early type of Chinese money shaped to look like a miniature spade. The background is similar to that of knife money.

STORE CARD: These were advertising tokens and coin substitutes. They were issued by the particular businessperson with the store's name and address on them. They were most popular in the United States during and immediately following the Civil War.

SUTLER'S TOKENS: Private individuals were given the right to sell canned goods, paper, envelopes, and numerous other items to soldiers just before and during the Civil War. The tokens they issued for use as change were known as sutler's tokens, as "sutler" was the name given to such a merchant. Later the sutlers were replaced with the now-familiar post exchanges (PX).

SWEATING COINS: This is a way of obtaining flecks of gold from coins without their being obviously reduced in metallic content. The gold coins are placed in a small container such as a box, then shaken together so they scrape one another. This removes flecks of the gold without being so obvious as the clipping technique. Given enough coins, the method could yield several dollars in gold beyond the face value of the coins being worn in this way.

TAEL: This term makes reference to one ounce of silver used by the Chinese. Later it came to mean a Chinese ounce measure that is slightly larger than the ounce used in the West.

TALENT: This was a weight that became a unit of value. It may have originally been valued at the same rate as an ox used in barter.

TOKEN: A coin-shaped piece of metal that is not authorized by the government. It might be used for advertising or as a money substitute during a coin shortage.

TRIAL PIECE: A coin that is struck during the preparation of the dies for regular coinage. Such pieces vary from a crude appearance to one that is close to the regular issues. Once the dies are ready for striking the regular coinage, no further trial pieces will be struck.

UNCIA: This was originally the ancient Roman ounce. Later it became a copper coin representing one-twelfth "as" or pound.

VECTURES: This is a term for tokens used to pay the fare for a bus, rapid transit, or other forms of transportation. A collector or student of this type of item is known as a vecturist.

WIRE MONEY: This is the Maundy money issued by George III in 1792. A peculiarity in the striking of the dates resulted in a wirelike appearance for some of the numbers.

WOODEN NICKELS: Although these "coins" are considered souvenir pieces by the people issuing them today, they were a true money substitute at one time. During the 1931–35 depression years, a number of communities struck wooden nickels for use when coins were in short supply.

YAP: This South Pacific Caroline Island is famous for a type of money known as fei, which seems to have been used since the Stone Age. Fei are large limestone disks ranging from six inches in diameter to twelve feet in diameter. They weigh several tons in their largest forms and apparently came from islands more than two hundred miles away. What their earliest uses may have been and how they were transported are mysteries today.

YEN: This is the standard money unit of Japan and is found in both silver and gold.

ZECCHINO: This is one of the first gold coins to be struck in medieval Europe. It was a ducat that originated in the palace called La Zecca, which served as the Venice Mint and also gave the coin its name. This type of coin first appeared in 1280 and continued to be struck until 1797.

BIBLIOGRAPHY

Amos, J. O. *Coin World Almanac.* Sidney, O.: Coin World, 1977.

Charlton, J. E. *A Standard Catalogue of Canadian Coins, Tokens and Paper Money.* Toronto, Ont., Canada: Charlton Publishing Company. Annually updated.

Clain-Stefanelli, E. and V. *The Beauty and Love of Coins, Currency and Medals.* New York: Riverwood Publishing Company, 1974.

Haffner, S. *The History of Modern Israel's Money.* Los Angeles, Calif.: La Mesa Publishing Company, 1968.

Reinfeld, F. *A Catalogue of the World's Most Popular Coins.* New York: Sterling Publishing Company, 1976.

Schwarz, Ted. *Coins as Living History.* New York: Arco Publishing Company, 1976.

Slabaugh, A. R. *United States Commemorative Coinage.* Chicago, Ill.: Albert Whitman & Company, 1977.

Taxay, Don. *Counterfeit, Mis-struck and Unofficial U.S. Coins.* New York: Arco Publishing Company, 1963.

————. *An Illustrated History of United States Commemorative Coinage.* New York: Arco Publishing Company, 1967.

————. *The United States Mint and Coinage— An Illustrated History from 1776 to Date.* New York: Arco Publishing Company, 1966.

Wear, T. G. *Ancient Coins: How to Collect for Fun and Profit.* Garden City, N.Y.: Doubleday & Company, 1965.

Yeoman, R. S. *A Guide Book of United States Coins.* Racine, Wis.: Western Publishing Company, 1976.